MARKET LEAD[ER]

International Management

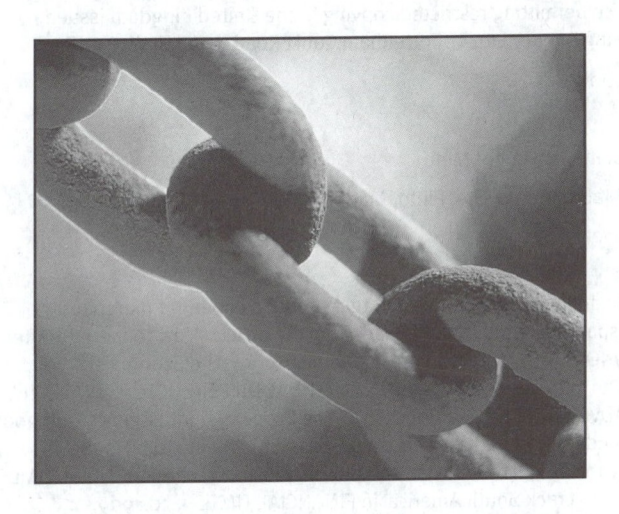

BUSINESS ENGLISH

Adrian Pilbeam

Longman

FINANCIAL TIMES
World business newspaper.

Pearson Education Limited
Edinburgh Gate, Harlow
Essex CM20 2JE, England
and Associated Companies throughout the World.
www.longman-elt.com
© Pearson Education Limited 2000

The rights of Adrian Pilbeam (*LTS Training and Consulting*) to be identified as the author of this work have been asserted by him in accordance with the Copyright, Designs and Patents Act 1988.

All rights reserved; no part of this publication may be reproduced, stored in a retrieval system, or transmitted in any form or by any means, electronic, mechanical, photocopying, recording, or otherwise without either the prior written permission of the Publishers or a licence permitting restricted copying in the United Kingdom issued by the Copyright Licensing Agency Ltd, 90 Tottenham Court Road, London W1P 9HE.

Third impression 2001

ISBN 0 582 328411

Set in 10/12.5pt Apolline, 10/12.5pt Meta

Printed in Spain by Mateu Cromo, S.A. Pinto, Madrid

www.market-leader.net

Acknowledgements

We are grateful to the following for permission to reproduce copyright material:
The Economist Newspaper Limited for an extract from the article 'How to merge – After the deal' in THE ECONOMIST 9.1.1999, © The Economist 1999; The Economist Intelligence Unit for an extract from MANAGING CULTURAL DIFFERENCES: STRATEGIES FOR COMPETITIVE ADVANTAGE by Lisa Hoecklin © The Economist Intelligence Unit 2000; Financial Times Limited for adapted extracts from: 'Case Study: Ford and Honda' in FINANCIAL TIMES 15.10.1997; 'Lowest cost isn't always the answer' in FINANCIAL TIMES 15.10.1997; 'Dell tries to crack South America' in FINANCIAL TIMES 5.10.1999; 'The e-lance economy' in FINANCIAL TIMES MASTERING INFORMATION MANAGEMENT 1.3.1999; 'Not to be taken for granted' in FINANCIAL TIMES 1.10.1999; 'Styles of execution' in FINANCIAL TIMES 23.2.1994; 'Star is reminder of proud auto heritage' in FINANCIAL TIMES 28.9.1999; 'The myth of the global executive' in FINANCIAL TIMES 8.10.1997; 'Don't forget the trailing spouse' in FINANCIAL TIMES 6.5.1998; the author Emma Haughton for an extract from the article 'What do employers say?' in THE INDEPENDENT 7.5.1998; The Irish Times for an extract from the article 'Doing the business' by Róisín Ingle in THE IRISH TIMES 8.3.1999; News Syndication International Limited for an extract from the article 'Industrialist honed by French polish' by Matthew Lynn in SUNDAY TIMES 22.11.1998, © Times Newspapers 1998; the author Robert Nurden for an extract from the article 'How to learn in a global classroom' in THE INDEPENDENT ON SUNDAY 25.4.1999; the author Joanna Parfitt, international journalist and expatriate specialist, for an extract from the article 'When it's time to come home' in THE INDEPENDENT ON SUNDAY 18.4.1999; Pearson Education Limited for an extract from MANAGING ACROSS CULTURES by Susan C Schneider and Jean-Louis Barsoux, © Prentice Hall Europe 1997 and Thomson Learning TM for the extract from INTERNATIONAL DIMENSIONS OF ORGANISATIONAL BEHAVIOUR 3rd edition by Nancy J Adler, 1997.

ASDA Stores Ltd for page 30 top; BMW AG for page 45 left; Daimler Chrysler for page 45 right; Ford Motor Company Ltd for page 9 left ; Honda for page 9 right; Unilever plc for page 62 and Wal-Mart for page 30 bottom.

Illustration acknowledgements

Nick Baker for 11, 43, 66; Jeremy Banx for 37; Katherine Walker for 38, 58.

Designed by Gemini Design

Project Managed by Chris Hartley

Contents

Part 1 BUSINESS STRATEGY

Unit 1	Company structure	4
Unit 2	The global company	8
Unit 3	Global production	12
Unit 4	Entering a foreign market	16
Unit 5	International mergers	20
Unit 6	Business in the 21st century	24

Part 2 CULTURAL ISSUES

Unit 7	Corporate cultures	28
Unit 8	Global careers	32
Unit 9	Management attitudes in Germany and Britain	36

Part 3 SELECTION, TRAINING AND DEVELOPMENT

Unit 10	The value of MBAs	40
Unit 11	Recruiting internationally	44
Unit 12	Selecting international managers	48
Unit 13	Training across cultures	52
Unit 14	International management development	56

Part 4 THE INTERNATIONAL MANAGER

Unit 15	Thinking global, acting local	60
Unit 16	Routes to top management	64
Unit 17	Overseas postings	68
Unit 18	Returning home	72

Glossary 76
Key 84
Check Tests 92
Check Tests Key 96

UNIT 1 Company structure

Before you read

Discuss these questions.
1 How many different ways of organising or structuring a company can you think of? Think about departments, products and markets.
2 If you work for a company or organisation, how would you describe the company structure?

Reading tasks

A Understanding main points

Read the text on the opposite page about the different ways in which companies are organised and answer these questions.
1 Four main kinds of organisational structure are described in the article. What are they?
2 Is one kind of organisational structure more common than the others?
3 When did 'delayering' take place?
4 What were the reasons for delayering and what were the results?
5 How does Julia MacLauchlan describe Microsoft's organisational structure?

B Understanding details

Match these definitions with the four organisational structures described in the text.
1 A cross-functional structure where people are organised into project teams.
2 A structure rather like the army, where each person has their place in a fixed hierachy.
3 A structure that enables a company to operate internationally, country by country.
4 A structure organised around different products.

C Understanding expressions

These words and expressions are used in the text to describe different aspects of organisational structure. Which are positive and which are negative?
1 clear lines of communication (line 32)   *positive*
2 bureaucratic set up (line 35)
3 speedy decision-making (line 36)
4 traditional hierarchical structure (line 77)
5 customercentric approach (line 91)
6 freedom to innovate (line 101)
7 flat organisational structure (line 107)

Doing the business

Róisín Ingle hears how efficient management structures are vital for success

The need for a solid structure within all business entities is 'absolutely fundamental', according to Ms Angela Tripoli, a lecturer in Business Administration at University College Dublin. 'Organisational structure concerns who reports to whom in the company and how different elements are grouped together. A new company cannot go forward without this and established companies must ensure their structure reflects their target markets, goals and available technology.'

Depending on their size and needs there are several organisational structures companies can choose from. Increasingly though, in the constantly evolving business environment, 'many firms are opting for a kind of hybrid of all of them'.

The most recognisable set up is called the *functional* structure where a fairly traditional chain of command (incorporating senior management, middle management and junior management) is put in place. The main benefit of this system is clear lines of communication from top to bottom but it is generally accepted that it can also be a bureaucratic set up which does not favour speedy decision-making.

More and more companies are organising themselves along *product* lines where companies have separate divisions according to the product that is being worked on. 'In this case the focus is always on the product and how it can be improved.'

The importance for multinational companies of a good *geographic* structure, said Ms Tripoli, could be seen when one electrical products manufacturer produced an innovative rice cooker which made perfect rice – according to western standards. When they tried to sell it on the Asian market the product flopped because there were no country managers informing them of the changes that would need to be made in order to satisfy this more demanding market.

The *matrix* structure first evolved during a project developed by NASA when they needed to pool together different skills from a variety of functional areas. Essentially the matrix structure organises a business into project teams, led by project leaders, to carry out certain objectives. Training is vitally important here in order to avoid conflict between the various members of the teams.

During the 1980s a wave of restructuring went through industry around the globe. This process, known as delayering, saw a change in the traditional hierarchical structures with layers of middle management being removed. This development was driven by new technology and by the need to reduce costs. The overall result was organisations that were less bureaucratic.

The delayering process has run its course now. Among the trends that currently influence how a company organises itself is the move towards centralisation and outsourcing. Restructuring has evolved along with a more 'customercentric' approach that can be seen to good effect in the banks. They now categorise their customers and their complex borrowing needs into groups instead of along rigid product lines.

Another development can be seen in larger companies, which are giving their employees more freedom to innovate in order to maintain a competitive edge.

Ms Julia MacLauchlan, Director of Microsoft's European Product Development Centre in Dublin, said the leading software company had a very flat organisational structure. 'There would not be more than around seven levels between the average software tester and Bill Gates,' she said.

Microsoft is a good example of a company that is structured along product lines. In Ireland, where 1,000 employees work on localisation of the software for all Microsoft's markets, the company is split up into seven business units. Each unit controls the localisation of their specific products while working closely with the designers in Microsoft's Seattle Headquarters.

It works, said Ms Maclauchlan, because everyone who works in the unit is 'incredibly empowered'.

'Without a huge bureaucratic infrastructure people can react a lot more quickly to any challenges and work towards the company's objectives.'

From *The Irish Times*

Company structure

Vocabulary tasks

A Collocations

Match these nouns as they occur together in the text.

1. product
2. target
3. borrowing
4. project
5. delayering
6. country
7. business
8. software
9. company

a) teams
b) objectives
c) lines
d) units
e) company
f) process
g) markets
h) needs
i) managers

B Complete the sentence

Use an appropriate phrase from Exercise A to complete each sentence.

1. Banks need to be fully aware of their customers' ...*borrowing needs*..... .
2. Silicon Valley is full of ....
3. Many companies are now organised along ...., in which each division is responsible for a group of products
4. A matrix organisation groups people into ....
5. Some companies are divided into different ...., often also called profit centres.
6. A multinational company will often have a number of ...., in charge of activities in different parts of the world.

C Definitions

Match these terms with their definitions.

1. business entities (line 2)
2. set up (line 25)
3. innovative (line 51)
4. flopped (line 55)
5. outsourcing (line 90)
6. customercentric (line 91)
7. competitive edge (line 102)

a) focusing on the customer rather than the product
b) new, original
c) companies
d) something that makes you better than other companies
e) did not succeed, failed
f) structure
g) getting external companies to do work for your company

D Prepositions

Complete these sentences with an appropriate preposition.

1 Organisational structure concerns who reports ....*to*......... whom.
2 Depending .... its size, there are several organisational structures a company can choose from.
3 Many companies are organising themselves .... product lines.
4 In the 1980s a wave of restructuring went .... industry.
5 Delayering was driven .... the need to reduce costs.
6 Microsoft in Ireland is split .... seven business units.

E Using a dictionary

A dictionary such as the *Longman Business English Dictionary* can help you to expand your vocabulary. Try these two exercises.

1 The word *business* is used several times in the article combined with another word which comes after it, e.g. *business environment* (line 21). It can also be combined with words that come before it, e.g. *big business*. Try to think of as many word combinations using *business* as you can, then look at the entry for *business* in the **Longman Business English Dictionary**.
2 Do the same exercise with the words *company, management, manager* and *product*.

Over to you

1 The functional organisational structure has clear lines of communication. In contrast, where things are organised along product lines or with a matrix structure, people often report to two people at the same time – their boss in the functional structure and their manager or team leader in the other structure. What, if any, problems could you imagine in the second case?

2 Do you think people from certain cultures would favour one kind of organisational structure over another? Can you think of some examples and give some reasons.

3 Either use your own company's organisational structure, or select one from a company's annual report, and give a presentation of it to your colleagues.

UNIT 2 The global company

Before you read

Discuss these questions.

1 Can there be such a thing as a 'world car'? Or should cars be designed to suit the tastes of different markets? What are the financial and marketing implications?
2 Which do you think is better for an international company – strong central control of international operations or decentralised decision-making? Does it depend on the business the company is in?

Reading tasks

A Understanding main points

1 Read the text on the opposite page about two car companies' global strategies and say which of these statements apply to Ford and which to Honda.
   a) now has a strategy of decentralisation   *Honda*
   b) now works in multi-disciplinary teams for car design and development
   c) has always worked in multi-disciplinary teams
   d) produces more cars abroad than in its home country
   e) used to be very decentralised
   f) used to be very centralised
   g) has divided the world into four regions
   h) designs and develops all its small cars in Europe
   i) has always been flexible and able to respond to change

2 According to the ideas in the text, why do car companies now need to have a global strategy?
3 How did the two companies change their strategies?

B How the text is organised

These phrases summarise the main idea of each paragraph of the text. Match each phrase with the correct paragraph.

a) one reason for changes in Honda's strategy
b) Honda's original strategy
c) Ford's new strategy
d) conclusion
e) Honda's new strategy
f) Ford's original strategy
g) the advantage of Honda's original strategy
h) introduction   *paragraph 1*
i) Ford's new strategy in detail
j) another reason for Honda's new strategy

Case study: Ford and Honda

Haig Simonian on two car groups' different routes to the global market

Rising costs and the worldwide spread of shared tastes in car styling have prompted the industry's giants to exploit global economies of scale. But rivals such as Ford and Honda have approached the task very differently.

Ford is one of the world's earliest multinationals. Its first foreign production unit was set up in Canada in 1904 – just a year after the creation of the US parent. For years Ford operated on a regional basis. Individual countries or areas had a large degree of autonomy from the US headquarters. That meant products differed sharply, depending on local executives' views of regional requirements. In Europe the company built different cars in the UK and Germany until the late 1960s.

Honda, by contrast, is a much younger company, which grew rapidly from making motorcycles in the 1950s. In contrast to Ford, Honda was run very firmly out of Japan. Until well into the 1980s, its vehicles were designed, engineered and built in Japan for sale around the world.

Significantly, however, Honda tended to be more flexible than Ford in developing new products. Rather than having a structure based on independent functional departments, such as bodywork or engines, all Japan's car makers preferred multi-disciplinary teams. That allowed development work to take place simultaneously, rather than being passed between departments. It also allowed much greater responsiveness to change.

In the 1990s both companies started to amend their organisational structures to exploit the perceived strengths of the other. At Ford, Alex Trotman, the newly appointed chairman, tore up the company's rulebook in 1993 to create a new organisation. The Ford 2000 restructuring programme threw out the old functional departments and replaced them with multi-disciplinary product teams.

The teams were based on five (now three) vehicle centres, responsible for different types of vehicles. Small and medium-sized cars, for example, are handled by a European team split between the UK and Germany. The development teams comprise staff from many backgrounds. Each takes charge of one area of the process, whether technical, financial or marketing-based.

Honda, by contrast, has decentralised in recent years. While its cars have much the same names around the world, they are becoming less, rather than more, standardised. 'Glocalisation' – a global strategy with local management – is the watchword. Eventually the group expects its structure will comprise four regions – Japan, the US, Europe and Asia-Pacific – which will become increasingly self-sufficient.

Two reasons explain Honda's new approach. Shifting to production overseas in the past decade has made the company more attuned to regional tastes. About 1m of Honda's 2.1m worldwide car sales last year were produced in the US. A further 104,000 were made in the UK. No other manufacturer has such a high proportion of foreign output.

Honda engineers also reckon they can now devise basic engineering structures which are common enough to allow significant economies of scale, but sufficiently flexible to be altered to suit regional variations. The US Accord, for example, is longer and wider than the Japanese version. The European one may have the same dimensions as the Japanese model, but has different styling and suspension settings.

Both Ford and Honda argue their new structures represent a correct response to the demands of the global market. Much of what they have done is similar, but intriguingly, a lot remains different.

FINANCIAL TIMES
World business newspaper.

The global company

Vocabulary tasks

A Synonyms

1 The word 'headquarters' (line 17) is used to describe the central, controlling part of a large, international company. What other word is used in the same paragraph with a similar meaning?
2 Honda and Ford manufacture cars. What other phrase is used to describe what they do?
3 Honda produces both cars and motorcycles. What is a general word for both of these?

B Word search

Find a word or phrase in the text that has a similar meaning.

1 when a company makes a product in big volumes to reduce costs (paras 1 and 9)
   e. *conomies*..... of s. *cale*............
2 factory in which cars are produced (para 2)
   p.................... u....................
3 independence (para 2)
   a....................
4 needs or demands (para 2)
   r....................
5 head of a company responsible for strategy rather than day-to-day management (para 5)
   c....................
6 consist of or be made up of (paras 6 and 7)
   c....................
7 financially independent (para 7)
   s....................-s....................
8 total of a company's production (para 8)
   o....................

C Complete the sentence

Use an appropriate word or phrase from Exercise B to complete each sentence.

1 The company ...*comprises*... three divisions – cars, trucks and commercial vehicles.
2 Each division has a lot of .... to decide its own strategy.
3 Companies seem to change their .... every few years in response to changing economic and market conditions.
4 Our total .... of cars from all our factories in Europe went down last year.
5 We need to develop products that meet the .... of the market.
6 Big car makers now produce different models based on the same platform in order to achieve ....
7 All the main Japanese car makers have .... in Europe.

D Expressing degrees of meaning

Complete these sentences with the adverb or phrase used in the text.

1. For many years Ford's products differed ....*sharply*..... from region to region.
2. Individual countries had .... of autonomy.
3. Honda grew .... from its early days as a motorcycle manufacturer.
4. For many years Honda was run very .... out of Japan.
5. The use of multi-disciplinary teams allowed development work at Honda to take place .... in different parts of the company.
6. Honda expects its four regions to become .... self-sufficient.
7. No other car maker has .... of foreign output as Honda.

Over to you

1. You have been asked by the board of a multinational car maker to present the case for a 'glocalisation' strategy, as described in the article. Prepare a presentation or write a report to give your arguments in favour of this.

2. You are members of the global strategy team of US Motors, an American multinational car maker. The company currently has production units in the UK, Germany, France and Spain for the European market. But with the opening up of the markets in Central and Eastern Europe, you are considering whether to set up a production unit in Poland. Hold a meeting to discuss the advantages and disadvantages of this strategy, and try to come to a decision.

UNIT 3

Global production

Before you read

Discuss these questions.

1 What criteria do you think global companies use when they choose the location of their manufacturing operations around the world? Some examples are labour costs, education level of the local workforce, and political stability. Can you think of others?

2 It has become increasingly common for organisations to subcontract some aspects of their activity to outside companies. Typical examples are catering (the company restaurant) or security (protecting the buildings). What, in your opinion, are the advantages and disadvantages of subcontracting work in this way?

Reading tasks

A Understanding main points

Read the text on the opposite page about how global companies organise their production and answer these questions.

1 Where are most simple toys manufactured and why?
2 Why does Lego do things differently?
3 What is the reason for a global company to have a 'part configuration' model?
4 According to the text, what are the advantages and disadvantages of 'low-cost assembly plants'?
5 What are the operational advantages of outsourcing?

B Understanding details

Mark these statements T (true) or F (false) according to the information in the text.
Find the part of the text that gives the correct information.

1 The main reason to have overseas plants is to be close to local markets. F
2 A lot of plants are now being located in Eastern Europe.
3 Imports to many markets are now cheaper.
4 The number of overseas plants is increasing.
5 Cost is the main factor in choosing the location of a foreign plant.
6 Outsourcing production to subcontractors gives a company more flexibility.

C How the text is organised

What do these words refer to in the text?

1 its (line 12)   *a global company*
2 its (line 17)
3 this (line 19)
4 this (line 36)
5 this (line 59)
6 it (line 93)

THE GLOBAL COMPANY

Lowest cost isn't always the answer

Lower tariffs and new markets opening to foreign investment have complicated the decision about how manufacturing should be organised, says **Nikki Tait**

Visit any western toy superstore, and most of the basic products will say 'Made in China' or, perhaps, Malaysia or Indonesia. Until, that is, you reach the Lego section. Suddenly, the boxes are more likely to identify Denmark, Switzerland or the US as the country of origin.

It might seem logical that a global company, selling into a multitude of country markets and measuring its market share in global terms, should place production facilities wherever costs are lowest. But Lego, the privately-owned Danish company, has for years concentrated its manufacturing in Europe and the US, arguing that this best satisfies design and quality requirements. For Lego the notion of cost is only a small part of the production picture.

So how does a global company go about organising its manufacturing network? The decision has become more complicated over the past two decades due to a number of factors. On the one hand, trade barriers across much of the world have declined sharply. Simultaneously, a range of new markets – notably in Asia and Eastern Europe – has opened to foreign investment.

This has made global production much more possible. But it has also reduced the need for many overseas plants. Markets that previously demanded local production facilities – because tariff levels made importing far too expensive – can now be supplied from other countries

Plainly, in this newly-liberalised environment, basic manufacturing costs do become more significant. But there are limits to a purely cost-driven approach. Many companies have built their current production structure through acquisitions over a number of years, rather than in a planned way.

Another problem is that costs themselves can be subject to rapid change, making today's Indonesia, for example, tomorrow's Hong Kong. This adds a further dimension to any global company's investment decision-making. The reality is that manufacturing businesses also need to think: how quickly can we pull the plug?

Some companies have addressed this issue through what is called the 'part configuration' model. This involves selecting a number of regional manufacturing bases which are viewed as longer-term investments, and augmenting them with lower-skilled assembly plants, which can more easily be moved between markets.

The availability of suitable employees also needs to be examined when investment decisions are being made. There may be close links between manufacturing and product innovation and if too much focus is put on low-cost assembly operations, product innovation tends to suffer.

Perhaps the hottest topic is whether a global company needs to be a producer at all. Outsourcing of production to other suppliers gives a company more flexibility, and fits well with a global strategy. A business may be better placed to supply differentiated products into different regional markets, and it can probably adjust more swiftly to changing cost considerations. These operational advantages come in addition to the financial benefits of outsourcing, such as lower capital employed.

But there can be pitfalls. Perhaps no company exemplifies the outsourcing trend better than Nike, the sports shoe group. On paper, its strategy of subcontracting the production of its shoes to local factories looks eminently sensible. But these arrangements have turned into a public relations disaster in recent years, as human rights campaigners have complained of 'sweatshop' conditions in many of the Asian plants producing Nike products. Lack of ownership, it seems, does not bring freedom from responsibility.

FINANCIAL TIMES
World business newspaper.

Global production

Vocabulary tasks

A Synonyms

1 The article deals with the question about where to locate 'production facilities'. Three other words are used in the article with a similar meaning to 'facilities'. What are they?

2 What other word is used in the article with the same meaning as 'production'?

B Word search

Find a word or phrase in the text that has a similar meaning.

1 amount in percentage terms of a company's sales compared to its competitors (para 2)
   m.*arket* s.*hare*

2 organisation of a company's production facilities around the world (para 3)
   m................ n................

3 legal or financial regulations to protect a country's domestic producers (para 3)
   t................ b................

4 amount of taxes on imports (para 4)
   t................ l................

5 strategy based mainly on keeping costs low (para 5)
   c................-d................ a................

6 companies bought as part of a strategy of expansion (para 5)
   a................

7 factory which puts together parts of a machine manufactured elsewhere (para 7)
   a................ p................

8 products that are specially prepared for different market needs (para 9)
   d................ p................

9 getting other companies to make products to your specification (para 9)
   o................

10 money invested in the business operations of a company (para 9)
    c................ e................

11 extremely bad working conditions, with low pay (para 10)
    s................ c................

C Definitions

Match these terms with their definitions.

1 notably (line 33)   a) is a typical example of something
2 augmenting (line 71)   b) especially, particularly
3 links (line 79)   c) a relationship or connection between two things
4 swiftly (line 94)   d) quickly
5 exemplifies (line 101)   e) very, extremely, completely
6 eminently (line 106)   f) increasing something by adding to it

D Complete the sentence

Use an appropriate word from Exercise C to complete each sentence.
1 The success of the engineering company ABB ..*exemplifies*.. the ability of an organisation to think globally and act locally.
2 We recruit our future international managers from the top business schools, ... Harvard, INSEAD and London.
3 Many business schools and management faculties have close .... with industry.
4 Our new Chief Executive was easily the best candidate for the job. In fact, he is .... suitable for this position.
5 During the busy months of the year we deal with the extra work by .... our full-time staff with temporary employees.
6 If incorrect and potentially damaging news is reported about the company in the press, it is important to move .... to deny it.

Over to you

1 Some of the main benefits for a company that is listed on the stock exchange are that it can raise capital by issuing new shares, and it can also use its own shares as payment when acquiring or taking over another company. But there are some disadvantages too. What do you think they are?

2 Most big international companies are listed on the stock market. But Lego is not. What do you think the reasons are?

3 Your company, a well known multinational producing components for the car industry, has a production plant in southern Italy, an area of high unemployment. The plant received Italian government and EU financial assistance when it was built three years ago. Now, due to poor productivity levels at the plant, the company is considering closing it down. However, there could be social, economic and political problems if it does so. You have been asked by the top management to write a report to present the case in favour of not closing it. Do so, giving as many reasons as you can.

4 You are a member of the strategic planning team of a company that produces PCs. Till now, the company has produced most of the components for the PCs itself. Hold a meeting to discuss the arguments for and against outsourcing the production of some of these components, so that your company becomes only an assembler and distributor of the finished PCs.

UNIT 4 Entering a foreign market

Before you read

Discuss these questions.

1 What are the main reasons for manufacturing a product in the country or region where you want to sell it?
2 A lot of products are increasingly being ordered by phone or through the Internet, assembled to order and delivered from the factory directly to the customer. This is especially the case in the US and Europe. Do you think this approach would work well in South America?

Reading tasks

A Understanding main points

Read the text on the opposite page about Dell's plans to assemble PCs in South America and answer these questions.

1 Is the writer generally positive about Dell's chances of success in its South American venture?
2 Why has Dell decided to attack the South American market?
3 Based on the information in the text, which country is the odd one out, and why?
   a) Colombia   b) Argentina   c) Brazil   d) Paraguay   e) Uruguay
4 Why has Dell chosen to locate its manufacturing plant in Brazil?
5 Which of the following 'challenges' facing Dell are mentioned in the article?
   a) unreliable transport networks ✓
   b) poor productivity
   c) political instability
   d) high inflation
   e) large distances
   f) high import tariffs
   g) terrorism
   h) well-established competitors

B Understanding details

Mark these statements T (true) or F (false) according to the information in the text. Find the part of the text that gives the correct information.

1 Dell will sell only in the big cities. F
2 Dell already sells computers in South America.
3 The company also produces PCs in Mexico.
4 It plans to import all the components it needs.
5 Ford and Volkswagen have been operating in South America for some years.
6 Considering South America as a single market is not an easy strategy.
7 To meet 'local content criteria' Dell must use a certain percentage of components produced locally.
8 Dell hopes to sell its computers duty-free in many countries.
9 Delivery systems in Brazil are better than in other parts of South America.

INFORMATION TECHNOLOGY LOGISTICS

Dell tries to crack South America

John Barham examines the US computermaker's strategy for expansion using a Brazillian base

Dell Computers, the Texas-based computer-maker that was among the pioneers of online ordering, is preparing to attack the difficult Latin American market.

Soon, Dell will start making computers at a new factory in the small, southern Brazilian city of Eldorado in its first manufacturing venture in South America. Within a few hours' flying time of Eldorado lie four of the continent's main metropolitan regions – Buenos Aires, Rio de Janeiro, Sao Paulo and Santiago – which generate about half the region's wealth and where most of the computer-using populace is concentrated. Dell hopes to serve all these markets – including more distant regions in northern Brazil and the Andean countries – from Eldorado.

According to Dell's plan, aircraft from Miami will land at a nearby international airport carrying computer components that will be sent straight to Dell's factory. Together with parts delivered from suppliers in Brazil, they will be assembled to order, packed and delivered to consumers across the continent.

The challenge for Dell is not only to mount an effective marketing campaign to educate customers about online ordering, it must also manage a complex logistics system and deal with the problems of unreliable road and air transport networks. And it must operate in half a dozen volatile Latin countries, with unpredictable governments and consumers as well as well-established competitors.

Dell could not afford to ignore the South American market much longer. It currently exports computers to a few Latin American countries such as Mexico and Colombia, but has never sold to markets in Argentina or Brazil. Latin American consumers last year bought 5 million PCs and demand is growing at 15 per cent a year. Growth is likely to remain strong for some time to come: in Brazil, the region's largest market, only 3–4 per cent of the population owns a PC.

Dell is not the first company to view South America as a single market. For a decade, Ford and Volkswagen and many other multinational companies have operated in the region's main countries as if they formed one integrated market. That was a natural reaction to falling import tariffs and consolidation of the Mercosur customs union linking Argentina, Brazil, Paraguay and Uruguay. However, the distances, the red tape and the animosities between national governments often make fulfilment of this strategy difficult.

Dell decided to locate in Brazil because it is the region's biggest market and because the government gives computer companies substantial tax incentives as part of its plan to develop local high technology industries. If Dell meets Brazilian local content criteria and attains agreed production volumes, its products are considered to be 100 per cent locally made and automatically gain duty-free access to Mercosur countries.

However, there is little Dell can do about the internal transport networks in Brazil or the bureaucracy in neighbouring countries. Although roads, air transport and delivery systems are tolerably efficient in south eastern Brazil and parts of Uruguay, Chile and Argentina, Dell may still find it is struggling to co-ordinate operations and sales over a vast region.

FINANCIAL TIMES
World business newspaper.

C Understanding details

Complete the sequence of steps in the planned assembly and delivery of Dell's PCs. (para 3)

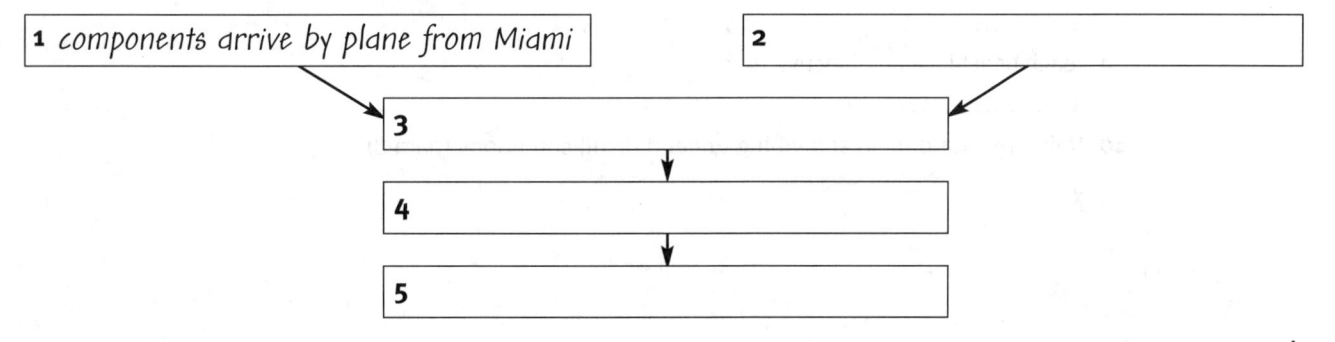

1 components arrive by plane from Miami

2

3

4

5

Entering a foreign market

D How the text is organised

These phrases summarise the main idea of each paragraph. Match each phrase to the correct paragraph.

- **a)** the challenge for Dell
- **b)** reason for choosing Brazil
- **c)** an overview of Dell's intentions   *paragraph 1*
- **d)** reason to enter the South American market.
- **e)** how Dell's plan will work
- **f)** other companies' experiences
- **g)** problems Dell may face in Brazil and elsewhere
- **h)** advantages of Eldorado's location

Vocabulary tasks

A Word search

Find a word or phrase in the text that has a similar meaning.

1. one of the first to do something (para 1)
   p. *ioneer*
2. buying something through the Internet (para 1)
   o.................. o...................
3. business activity with some element of risk (para 2)
   v..................
4. general population in a country (para 2)
   p..................
5. a difficult task which needs skill and determination (para 4)
   c..................
6. describes something or someone that can change quickly and suddenly (para 4)
   v..................
7. lots of rules and regulations, which often seem to have no purpose (para 6)
   r.................. t..................
8. strong dislike between people or groups (para 6)
   a..................
9. reach or achieve an objective (para 7)
   a..................
10. trying very hard to do something under difficult conditions (para 8)
    s..................

B Collocations

1 Match these nouns as they occur together in the text.
   a) tax — venture
   b) manufacturing — incentives
   c) import — system
   d) customs — tariffs
   e) production — volumes
   f) logistics — union

2 Match these verbs and nouns as they occur in the text.
   a) mount — access
   b) serve — criteria
   c) generate — a campaign
   d) gain — a market
   e) meet — wealth

C Complete the sentence

Use an appropriate phrase from Exercise B to complete each sentence.

1 Many countries offer companies ..*tax incentives*.. to encourage inward investment.
2 When we launch our new Internet service we will need to .... a big marketing ....
3 In order to be successful, the new manufacturing plant will have to reach target .... within six months.
4 Assembling to order and delivering direct to each customer means managing a complex ....
5 When importing is expensive due to high .... , the alternative is to manufacture locally.
6 In order to have free access to the EU market, Japanese car manufacturers in the UK need to .... minimum content ....
7 In some countries the only way to .... well is to have local production.
8 Most countries in Europe are now part of a .... which allows free movement of goods.

Over to you

1 Imagine you work in the marketing department of a European truck manufacturer. Prepare a presentation giving arguments for setting up production in South America.

2 You are a consultant specialising in economic and political fields. You have been asked by a client, a European computer manufacturer, to summarise in a report the difficulties and challenges of setting up a production operation in one of the following countries: Colombia, Russia or Indonesia. Choose one and write a report.

UNIT 5 International mergers

Before you read

Discuss these questions.
1 How would you define a merger? How does it differ from an acquisition?
2 Think of three or four big international mergers in recent years. Have they been successful?
3 What kind of things do you think can lead to problems or even failure in international mergers and acquisitions?

Reading tasks

A Understanding main points

Mark these statements T (true) or F (false) according to the information in the text on the opposite page. Find the part of the text that gives the correct information.
1 The majority of mergers take place in the USA. F
2 Many international mergers are failures.
3 Most attention is concentrated on what to do after the merger is completed.
4 Many mergers are done too quickly.
5 Connecting different computer systems together is not usually a problem.
6 High salaries were given to Chrysler managers as compensation for the merger with Daimler-Benz.
7 Chrysler has won many prizes for its production methods.
8 Engineers have a high status at Daimler-Benz.

B Understanding expressions

Choose the best explanation for each extract from the text.
1 'the merger wave is now sweeping over Europe' (line 1)
   a) a lot of American companies are merging with European ones
   b) there has been a big increase in the number of mergers involving European companies
2 'success will depend on the merged companies' ability to create added value' (line 18)
   a) they must try to make sure the share price goes up after the merger
   b) they must try to reduce costs and increase revenue in the new merged company
3 'post-merger integration has become decisive' (line 31)
   a) the way merged companies work together as one company is extremely important
   b) it is necessary to take quick decisions after the merger is competed
4 'the growing importance of intangible assets' (line 63)
   a) some assets are carefully protected and cannot be touched
   b) people are the most valuable asset in many companies

International mergers

HOW TO MERGE

After the deal

Doing deals is easy. As mergers hit record levels, now comes the hard part

The merger wave, which in 1998 was a predominantly American affair, is now sweeping over Europe. Cross-border deals, such as Daimler-Benz's takeover of Chrysler, accounted for a quarter of mergers in 1998; more are expected as firms go global.

In many cases this consolidation makes sense – at least on paper. But just as certain as the flow of deals is that most will be failures. Study after study of past merger waves has shown that two out of every three deals have not worked.

Success in the future will depend more than ever on the merged companies' ability to create added value. And that will depend mainly on what happens after the deal has been done. Yet many deal makers have neglected this side of the business. Once the merger is done, they simply assume that computer programmers, sales mangers and engineers will cut costs and boost revenue according to plan.

Yet, just when post-merger integration has become decisive, it has become harder to pull off. Not only are modern firms complicated global affairs, but executives are putting today's deals together in a hurry. Few give enough thought to the pitfalls.

One set of obstacles is 'hard' things, such as linking distribution or computer systems. In particular, many recent mergers have been undone by the presumption that information technology is easy to mesh together.

More difficult are the 'soft issues'; and here the same word keeps popping up – culture. People never fit together as easily as flow charts. Culture permeates a company, and differences can poison any collaboration. After one large US merger, the two firms had a row over the annual picnic: employees of one company were accustomed to inviting spouses, the others were totally against the idea. The issue was resolved by inviting spouses only in alternate years.

Two new things have made culture clashes harder to manage. The first is the growing importance of intangible assets. In an advertising agency, for instance, most of the value can walk out of the door if key people leave.

The second new thing is the number of cross-border mergers. In this area DaimlerChrysler may prove to be an interesting case study in differing management cultures. One worry is compensation: Chrysler's pay levels are much higher than the German company's. So a US manager posted to Stuttgart may end up reporting to a German manager who is earning half his salary.

Nor is pay the only difference. Chrysler likes to pride itself on its flexible approach, where speed and ingenuity are prized. When designing new models, teams of engineers, designers and marketing people work on each model. Daimler-Benz has a more traditional structure, in which designers and marketing people mix less and engineers are in charge.

Some recent deals will no doubt prove a stunning success. Nevertheless, there are three ominous signs about the current merger boom. First, much of the attention seems to be on the deal itself rather than the integration that must follow. Second, many deals are rushed. And third, mergers have too often become a strategy in their own right.

So the things that are so impressive about today's mergers – their size, complexity and daring – could count against them if the economy turns down.

From *The Economist*

C How the text is organised

What do these words refer to in the text?

1 which (line 1)   *merger wave*
2 more (line 8)
3 most (line 13)
4 that (line 21)
5 this (line 25)
6 they (line 26)
7 it (line 32)
8 few (line 37)

International mergers

Vocabulary tasks

A Word search

Find a word or phrase in the text that has a similar meaning.

1. mergers between companies from two different countries (para 1)
   c. ross -b. order d. eals

2. when one company buys another (para 1)
   t...................

3. when a company becomes more international (para 1)
   g................... g...................

4. people who negotiate the terms of a merger (para 3)
   d................... m...................

5. reduce the amount of money spent (para 3)
   c................... c...................

6. increase income from sales (para 3)
   b................... r...................

7. work that needs to be done after the merger agreement (para 4)
   p...................-m................... i...................

8. sent to a job in another country (para 8)
   p...................

B Understanding expressions

Choose the best explanation for each word or phrase from the text.

1. pull off (line 33)
   a) stop
   b) succeed ✓

2. pitfalls (line 38)
   a) problems
   b) accidents

3. mesh together (line 45)
   a) combine
   b) mix up

4. popping up (line 48)
   a) exploding
   b) coming up

5. permeates (line 50)
   a) destroys permanently
   b) goes into every part

6 pride itself (line 81)
  a) be pleased with yourself for something
  b) tell everyone about your good points
7 ominous (line 93)
  a) easy to predict
  b) predicting something bad
8 in their own right (line 101)
  a) by themselves
  b) in a correct way

C Prepositions

Complete these sentences with an appropriate preposition.

1 Cross-border deals accounted ....*for*........ a quarter of mergers in 1998.
2 Two .... every three deals have not worked.
3 Success will depend .... the merged companies' ability to create added value.
4 They assume sales managers and engineers will cut costs according .... plan.
5 Executives are putting deals together .... a hurry.
6 Employees of one company were accustomed .... inviting spouses to the annual picnic.
7 An American manager may report .... a German boss.
8 In Daimler-Benz, engineers are .... charge.

Over to you

1 The article emphasises that the post-merger integration is the hardest but most important part of the deal. Here is a list of some issues that must be considered to enable things to work well after a merger has taken place. Which are the most important? Can you add others? What factors need to be taken into account when coming to decision?
   - who will be the chief executive of the new company?
   - where will the HQ be?
   - if it is a merger between companies from different countries with different languages, what should the company language be?
   - on which stock exchange should the new company be listed?
   - where there is duplication, e.g. two centres for R&D, should one be closed?
   - should key managers be moved to different parts of the merged company to speed up integration?

2 Differences in pay levels between the two companies in a merger can cause problems. Imagine you are members of the Human Resources departments of the two companies. Hold a meeting to discuss this problem and try to suggest some solutions.

UNIT 6 Business in the 21st century

Before you read

Discuss these questions.
1 What impact are developments in information technology having on the way companies are organised, e.g. the use of video conferencing, which means people need to travel less?
2 How has the Internet changed the way you work or study?

Reading tasks

A Understanding main points

Read the text on the opposite page about how businesses will be organised in the future and answer these questions.
1 Which of these statements gives the best summary of the ideas in the article?
   a) New communications technologies enable information to be shared instantly across the world.
   b) In the future most people will be self-employed or will work as freelancers.
   c) Companies are having to restructure due to developments in electronic communications.
2 What exactly do the authors mean by the term 'e-lance economy'?
   a) Most work inside large companies will be done using e-mail and computers.
   b) In the future tasks will be done by individuals and small companies linked to the Internet.
   c) Business between companies will increasingly be done through the Internet.

B Understanding details

Mark these statements T (true) or F (false) according to the information in the text. Find the part of the text that gives the correct information.
1 Big corporations will soon go out of business. F
2 There is a move towards decentralisation of decision-making in many companies.
3 Many companies are now experiencing cash flow and similar financial problems.
4 No more than 10 per cent of workers in the US work for the top 500 companies.
5 ABB and BP Amoco have sold many parts of their businesses.
6 Large organisations can save money by centralising all transactions.
7 Computer companies have decentralised their decision-making process.
8 It is possible that the shape and structure of companies will be very different in the future.

The e-lance economy

Summary

Despite the wave of big mergers and acquisitions over the past few years, the days of the big corporation - as we know it - are numbered. While the cash flows that they control are growing, the direct power that they exercise over actual business processes is declining. Because modern communications technology makes decentralised organisations possible, control is being passed down the line to workers at many different levels, or outsourced to external companies. In fact, we are moving towards what can be called an 'e-lance economy', which will be characterised by shifting coalitions of freelancers and small firms using the Internet for much of their work.

Twenty-five years ago, one in five US workers was employed by one of the top 500 companies. Today, the ratio has dropped to fewer than one in ten. Large companies are far less vertically integrated than they were in the past and rely more and more on outside suppliers to produce components and provide services, with a consequent reduction in the size of their workforce.

At the same time, decisions within large corporations are increasingly being pushed to lower levels. Workers are rewarded not for carrying out orders efficiently, but for working out what needs to be done and doing it. Many large industrial companies – ABB and BP Amoco are among the most prominent – have broken themselves up into numerous independent units that transact business with one another almost as if they were separate companies.

What underlies this trend? The answer lies in the basic economics of organisations. Business organisations are, in essence, mechanisms for co-ordination, and the form they take is strongly affected by the co-ordination technologies available. When it is cheaper to conduct transactions internally, with other parts of the same company, organisations grow larger, but when it is cheaper to conduct them externally, with independent entities in the open market, organisations stay small or shrink.

The co-ordination technologies of the industrial era – the train and the telegraph, the car and the telephone, the mainframe computer and the fax machine – made transactions within the company not only possible but advantageous. Companies were able to manage large organisations centrally, which provided them with economies of scale in manufacturing, marketing, distribution and other activities. Big was good.

But with the introduction of powerful personal computers and electronic networks – the co-ordination technologies of the 21st century – the economic equation changes. Because information can be shared instantly and inexpensively among many people in many locations, the value of centralised decision-making and bureaucracy decreases. Individuals can manage themselves, co-ordinating their efforts through electronic links with other independent parties. Small becomes good.

In the future, as communications technologies advance and networks become more efficient, the shift to e-lancing promises to accelerate. Should this happen, the dominant business organisation of the future may not be a stable, permanent corporation but rather a flexible network of individuals and small groups that might sometimes exist for no more than a day or two. We will enter the age of the temporary company.

FINANCIAL TIMES
World business newspaper.

C How the text is organised

These phrases summarise the purpose of each paragraph. Match each phrase to the correct paragraph.

a) illustrate the decline of big companies   *paragraph 1*
b) give a prediction about the future
c) give examples of changes in the way big companies are organised
d) introduce the idea that big companies are starting to change and even decline   *summary*
e) describe the new way of working
f) explain why these changes are taking place
g) describe the old way of working

Business in the 21st century

Vocabulary tasks

A Word search

1 Find a word or phrase from the text that has a similar meaning.
   a) movement of money into and out of a company's bank accounts (summary)
      c..*ash*........ f..*low*............
   b) passing tasks to an external company (summary)
      o....................
   c) individuals who are self-employed and work independently (summary)
      f....................
   d) describes a large company that produces everything it needs internally (para 1)
      v.................... i....................
   e) external companies that provide products or services to an organisation (para 1)
      o.................... s....................
   f) parts of a company that operate independently as separate profit centres (para 2)
      i.................... u....................
   g) where price and quality are the main factors for doing business (para 3)
      o.................... m....................
   h) something large companies can achieve by doing things in big volumes (para 4)
      e.................... of s....................

2 There are many words that can be used instead of 'company'. Four other words are used in the text. What are they? Is there any difference in meaning between them?

B Understanding expressions

Choose the best explanation for each phrase from the text.

1 'the days of the big corporation are numbered' (line 2)
   a) big companies will become less important in the future ✓
   b) companies will have to improve their financial controls
2 'control is being passed down the line' (line 6)
   a) nobody in the company wants to take decisions
   b) some decisions will be taken at lower levels in the company
3 'what underlies this trend?' (line 37)
   a) is this trend really true?
   b) what are the reasons for this trend?
4 'in essence' (line 40)
   a) basically
   b) necessarily

26

5 'organisations shrink' (line 51)

   a) they become smaller

   b) they disappear completely

   6 'the economic equation changes' (line 70)

   a) things become cheaper because of the Internet

   b) there is a move in favour of decentralisation

C Complete the sentence

Use an appropriate verb and preposition to complete each sentence.

1. Large multinationals still e.*xercise*......... considerable power o.*ver*............... many people around the world.
2. It's a difficult problem. It will take time to w.................. o................... the best way to solve it.
3. In a traditional, hierarchical company, employees are expected to c.................. o.................. the orders of their superiors.
4. To improve flexibility and speed of reaction we have decided to b.................. the company u................... into separate business units.
5. Our policy is to t................... business only w................... companies that have a strong environmental policy.
6. The speed at which you can get information from the Internet is sometimes a................... b................... the time of day.

Over to you

1. Do you agree with the opinions in the article? Can you give some examples from real cases to support your opinion?

2. The authors are both on the academic staff of MIT (The Massachusetts Institute of Technology) in the USA. Till now, most of the innovations in using the Internet and in 'e-commerce' have come from the USA, where companies seem prepared to use new technology quickly. Do you think that the concept of the 'e-lance economy' described in the article is mainly relevant to the USA or do you think it will work in other parts of the world too?

3. If what the authors write is true, what are the implications for the way international managers will need to work in the future and also for the training and education they will need?

UNIT 7 Corporate cultures

Before you read

Discuss these questions.

1 Every organisation has its own distinctive culture, and this can vary enormously from company to company. To an outsider, corporate culture differences are usually reflected in external symbols or characteristics, such as advertising and design. Other characteristics of corporate culture are only observable when you get inside the company as an employee or a supplier, such as the kind of dress worn by staff or the use of first names. Try to think of some other characteristics of corporate culture based on companies that you know.

2 Think of some large supermarket groups you know. What kind of image do they project to their customers, e.g. friendly, giving best value?

Reading tasks

A Understanding main points

Read the text on the opposite page about the merger of two companies and their corporate cultures and answer these questions.

1 Which company is bigger – Asda or Wal-Mart?
2 What are employees at Asda called?
3 Which two countries are Asda and Wal-Mart from?
4 Which of these statements best summarises the corporate cultures of Asda and Wal-Mart?
   a) We must keep costs as low as possible.
   b) We value the contribution of every employee to the success of the company.
   c) Everyone in the company is considered equal.
5 What extra financial benefit do Wal-Mart employees have?
6 Allan Leighton mentions three things needed to get the deal 'to work culturally'. What are they?

B Understanding details

Mark these statements T (true) or F (false) according to the information in the text.
Find the part of the text that gives the correct information.

1 Asda and Wal-Mart have very similar corporate cultures. T
2 Asda is the biggest supermarket group in the UK.
3 Wal-Mart is the biggest retailing group in the US.
4 Asda had financial problems in the 1980s.
5 Many of Asda's employees are over 65.
6 Allan Leighton is sure the merger of Asda with Wal-Mart will succeed.
7 Wal-Mart plans to impose its corporate culture on Asda.
8 Creating a corporate culture cannot be planned in theory only.

Corporate cultures

TRANSPOSING A CULTURE by Peggy Hollinger

Not to be taken for granted

Asda and Wal-Mart should be the perfect merger, given that the former has deliberately set out to copy the US retailing giant's style. But Asda is keenly aware of the pitfalls.

You could not hope to find a neater fit, said the commentators when Wal-Mart, the world's biggest retailer, agreed a £6.7bn takeover deal with Asda, the UK's number three supermarket group.

It had long been known that the team which was brought in to rescue Asda from collapse in the mid-1980s had deliberately set out to copy virtually every aspect of the giant US discount group that could be replicated in the UK.

So Asda stores have 'colleagues', not employees. They have people in the parking lots to help drivers to park. They have old-age pensioners wearing colourful name badges, standing at the door to say hello and ask customers if they need help. In the Leeds headquarters no one has an individual office, not even the chairman. Finally, store staff get actively involved in promoting individual product lines, and are rewarded when their efforts lead to tangible sales improvements.

Most of these ideas came straight from Bentonville, Arkansas, home to one of the world's most unusual retailers. For Wal-Mart's corporate culture has become a legend in retailing.

The company's employees chant the Wal-Mart cheer before store meetings. They benefit from a share ownership scheme which is one of the most widespread in the industry. Top executives share rooms when on business trips, and pay for their coffee and tea from vending machines like the lowliest sales assistant.

Given the similarities, there are few who really believe putting Asda into the Wal-Mart network will result in anything but success. But, says Asda's Chief Executive, Allan Leighton, this is no reason to be complacent. Failing to bring together corporate cultures, even those as similar as Asda's and Wal-Mart's, could lead to the downfall of the most logical mergers. 'When acquiring or merging with a business, getting the cultures to fit is fundamentally important,' he says. Half-way houses, where compromises are made, never work, he believes, and nor does imposing one culture on another. 'A company calling their colleagues colleagues and treating them like staff is not the answer,' he says.

The key to getting the deal to work culturally rests on a few fundamental issues, he believes. The first and most important is terminology, he says. 'Businesses have their own language. You have to get everyone aligned so that when someone uses a word it means the same thing to everyone.'

Middle management comes next. 'Initially, everything is done at the top of the organisation,' he says. 'But most of the work is done in the middle.' If middle management is not incentivised, a deal can go horribly wrong. 'It all boils down to people in the end. And what motivates people? Unless you can demonstrate very quickly that their influence in the organisation is at least the same if not better than before, then people will get concerned about it,' he says.

Third comes getting to know each other. Asda and Wal-Mart have spent the last few weeks swapping store managers and IT systems staff. 'We will go out there, look and bring back,' Leighton says. 'That way we will have ownership of the changes as opposed to having them pushed on us.'

It will always be hard to determine whether a merger or takeover has failed because the cultures simply did not fit. But success is more likely to elude those who do not really believe in the cultures they are trying to create. 'This all comes from the heart,' says Leighton. 'You do not get it from textbook management or instruction. You have to create an environment where people feel comfortable in expressing themselves in a different way.'

FINANCIAL TIMES
World business newspaper.

C Understanding meanings

1. Choose the best explanation of the phrase 'there are few who really believe putting Asda into the Wal-Mart network will result in anything but success' (line 45)

    a) most people think the combination of Asda and Wal-Mart will succeed

    b) not many people think the merger will succeed

2. What does Allan Leighton mean when he says 'it all boils down to people in the end' (line 81)

    a) the number of people in the new organisation will need to be reduced

    b) people are the most important element in a merger or takeover

Corporate cultures

Vocabulary tasks

A Synonyms

1. The word 'employees' is used several times in the text. What other word is used that has a similar meaning? (para 3)
2. The phrase 'to push something on someone' is used in line 97. What similar phrase is used earlier in the text? (para 6)

B Word search

Find a word or phrase in the text that has a similar meaning.

1. agreement when a company buys another (para 1)
   t.*akeover*........ d.*eal*..............
2. when a company fails (para 2)
   c...................
3. something that is copied exactly (para 2)
   r...................
4. something that can be seen and proved (para 3)
   t...................
5. company that is famous in its industry (para 4)
   l...................
6. being unreasonably confident (para 6)
   c...................
7. agreement where both sides give up some of what they want (para 6)
   c...................
8. in the same position or share the same ideas (para 7)
   a...................
9. exchanging people or things (para 9)
   s...................

C Definitions

Match these terms with their definitions.

1. virtually (line 11)
2. parking lots (line 16)
3. old-age pensioners (line 17)
4. chant (line 35)
5. widespread (line 39)
6. lead to the downfall (line 54)
7. incentivised (line 80)
8. elude (line 102)

a) cause something to fail
b) people of retirement age who no longer work
c) almost all
d) sing
e) escape
f) a place where cars are put
g) motivated through money or other means
h) available to lots of people

D Collocations

Match these nouns as they occur together in the text.

1. IT
2. product
3. name
4. store
5. sales
6. share
7. middle
8. business

a) ownership
b) trip
c) systems
d) line
e) management
f) badges
g) assistant
h) manager

E Complete the sentence

Use an appropriate phrase from Exercise D to complete each sentence.

1. ......*Share ownership*......... schemes for employees help to develop loyalty and commitment.
2. Most large supermarkets sell hundreds of ....
3. With the increased emphasis on the customer in retailing, the role of the .... is important.
4. The increased use of audio and video conferencing should reduce the number of .... executives need to make.
5. Large organisations need sophisticated .... to operate efficiently.
6. If people didn't wear .... at big conferences, you wouldn't know who anyone was.
7. Most executives never progress beyond ....
8. The role of a .... is to motivate and control the sales staff in the shop.

Over to you

1. Wal-Mart's corporate culture 'has become a legend in retailing'. It includes such things as employees chanting the Wal-Mart cheer each day before the store opens. How well do you think Wal-Mart's corporate culture would 'travel' across national cultures, especially outside the UK and the US? Would you feel comfortable with it?

2. Choose two large retailing, restaurant or hotel groups that you are familiar with. If you have time, go and observe the way they present themselves to customers. Then give a presentation comparing the two organisations' approaches to customers.

UNIT 8 Global careers

Before you read

Discuss these questions.

1. What qualities do you think a person needs in order to be a successful global manager? Some examples may be independence, or an interest in foreign cultures. Try to think of others.
2. What personal and professional skills do you need for a successful business career in your country, e.g. specialist training, knowledge of foreign languages, outgoing personality?

Reading tasks

A Understanding main points

1. Which of these statements gives the best summary of the text on the opposite page?
   a) A successful global manager needs many qualities.
   b) The qualities required to become a top manager differ from country to country.
   c) Many young managers are not interested in a global career.

2. Mark these statements T (true) or F (false) according to the information in the text. Find the part of the text that gives the correct information.
   a) International experience is essential if you want a global career.
   b) Subsidiaries of global companies use the same criteria when promoting managers.
   c) The demand for global managers is increasing.
   d) Young managers want to work internationally.

B Understanding details

1. Different qualities for career success are described for different cultures and nationalities. Match the qualities from the list below to the nationalities mentioned in the text.
   a) good communication skills   *British*
   b) technical creativity
   c) ability to network
   d) professional competence
   e) entrepreneurial skills
   f) knowing how to work within a hierarchical structure
   g) good interpersonal skills

2. Which national group considers communication and interpersonal skills to be more important – the British or the Dutch?

3. According to André Laurent, German, British and French managers see organisations as different kinds of networks. What words does he use to define these networks in each case?

Global Careers

Ideally, it seems a global manager should have the stamina of an Olympic runner, the mental agility of an Einstein, the conversational skill of a professor of languages, the detachment of a judge, the tact of a diplomat, and the perseverance of an Egyptian pyramid builder. And that's not all. If they are going to measure up to the demands of living and working in a foreign country, they should also have a feeling for the culture; their moral judgement should not be too rigid; they should be able to merge with the local environment; and they should show no signs of prejudice.

Thomas Aitken

According to Colby Chandler, the former Chief Executive of Eastman Kodak Company, 'these days there is not a discussion or a decision that does not have an international dimension. We would have to be blind not to see how critically important international experience is.'

International companies compete with each other for global executives to manage their operations around the world. Yet what it takes to reach the top of a company differs from one country to the next. For example, whereas Swiss and German companies respect technical creativity and competence, French and British companies often view managers with such qualities as 'mere technicians'. Likewise, American companies value entrepreneurs highly, while their British and French counterparts often view entrepreneurial behaviour as highly disruptive. Similarly, whereas only just half of Dutch managers see skills in interpersonal relations and communication as critical to career success, almost 90 per cent of their British colleagues do so.

Global management expert, André Laurent, describes German, British and French managers' attitudes to management careers as follows:

German managers, more than others, believe that creativity is essential for career success. In their mind, successful managers must have the right individual characteristics. German managers have a rational outlook; they view the organisation as a co-ordinated network of individuals who make appropriate decisions based on their professional competence and knowledge.

British managers hold a more interpersonal and subjective view of the organisational world. According to them, the ability to create the right image and to get noticed for what they do is essential for career success. British managers view organisations primarily as a network of relationships between individuals who get things done by influencing each other through communicating and negotiating.

French managers look at organisations as an authority network where the power to organise and control others comes from their position in the hierarchy. French managers focus on the organisation as a pyramid of differentiated levels of power. They perceive the ability to manage power relationships effectively and to 'work the system' as critical to their career success.

As companies integrate their operations globally, these different national approaches can send conflicting messages to success-oriented managers. Subsidiaries in different countries operate differently and reward different behaviours based on their unique cultural perspectives. The challenge for today's global companies is to recognise local differences, while at the same time creating globally integrated career paths for their future senior executives.

There is no doubt the new global environment demands more, not fewer, globally competent managers. Global experience, rather than side-tracking a manager's career, is rapidly becoming the only route to the top. But in spite of the increasing demand for global managers, there is a potentially diminishing interest in global assignments, especially among young managers. A big question for the future is whether global organisations will remain able to attract sufficient numbers of young managers willing to work internationally.

From *International Dimensions of Organisational Behaviour,* Thomson Learning 1997

Global careers

D Understanding meanings

1. Choose the best explanation of the sentence 'there is not a discussion or a decision that does not have an international dimension' (line 8)?
   a) international issues are not often discussed when companies take decisions
   b) international issues must always be considered when taking a business decision

2. Choose the best explanation of the phrase 'mere technicians' (line 13) as it is used in the text?
   a) people who have some technical skills but no management skills
   b) people who are excellent engineers

Vocabulary tasks

A Definitions

Match these terms with their definitions.

1. stamina — a) ability to think quickly and intelligently
2. mental agility — b) physical or mental strength to continue doing something
3. detachment — c) ability to be polite and careful in what you say or do
4. tact — d) determination to keep trying to do something difficult
5. perseverance — e) not becoming involved in things emotionally

B Word search

Find a word or phrase in the text that has a similar meaning.

1. behaviour which prevents things from working normally (para 3)
   d. isruptive ...... b. ehaviour ......
2. managers who are ambitious (para 8)
   s.............-o............ m................
3. clear directions that people can follow to move up in a company (para 8)
   c............... p.................
4. push a manager's career into a dead end (para 9)
   s..............-t...............
5. when interest is becoming less and less (para 9)
   d............... i...................

C Prepositions

Match the verbs and prepositions as they occur together in the text.

1. based — a) up to
2. compete — b) on
3. have a feeling — c) from
4. differ — d) with
5. measure — e) for

D Complete the sentence

Use an appropriate phrase from Exercise C to complete each sentence.

1 German managers take decisions ...*based on*.... their professional knowledge.
2 The qualities most valued in managers .... country to country.
3 To operate successfully in different countries you need to .... good .... different cultures.
4 In a global company, managers from different countries .... each other for the top jobs.
5 Expatriates who don't .... to the demands of working and living abroad sometimes return from their foreign assignment early.

Over to you

1 Do you agree with the list of personal qualities necessary to be a global manager which are quoted by Thomas Aitken at the beginning of the text? Can you add anything?

2 If you have experience of companies in Germany, Britain and France, would you agree with André Laurent's analysis of what is essential for career success and how organisations work in each country? Can you add anything?

3 Imagine that you wish to apply for the job advertised below. You have the right qualifications and experience, and these are on your CV. Write a letter of application to accompany your CV, emphasising your personal qualities and suitability for this position.

European Management Journal
Director, International Sales & Marketing

As a key member of our managerial team, you will direct the international business, promotional, and advertising sales activities for The European Management Journal. You will determine the profitability and feasibility of establishing new products and build strategies for delivering current products into new international markets. You will also direct an independent sales force on three continents and be responsible for the day-to-day management and co-ordination of marketing strategies between national and international divisions.

Requires a BA (or equivalent) in Marketing or Finance, and 7 years' product management or development experience, with 3+ years' international marketing/sales experience in publishing or management development. An MBA, experience in start up ventures, and the ability to adapt to different cultures preferred. English and one other European language essential. Overseas travel is required. The post is based in Brussels.

UNIT 9 Management attitudes in Germany and Britain

Before you read

Discuss these questions.

1 What is the 'message' of the cartoon on the opposite page?
2 Based on your experience or what you may have read, how do you think British and German managers would differ in their approach to management?

Reading tasks

A Understanding main points

1 The text on the opposite page describes two main differences between British and German management. What are they?
2 Mark these statements T (true) or F (false) according to the information in the text. Find the part of the text that gives the correct information.
   a) Mergers between British and German companies rarely succeed. *F*
   b) The study mainly concentrated on middle managers.
   c) Both German and British managers consider technical skills to be very important.
   d) German managers prefer working with technicians in British companies.
   e) British managers are very concerned about their executive status.
   f) There is much more change in British companies than in German companies.
   g) German companies are strong and successful because of the way they are organised.
   h) British managers are probably more flexible than their German counterparts.
3 In your opinion does the article suggest that one country's approach to management and organisation is better than the other's?
4 Pick out some extracts from the article which make positive or negative comments about British or German approaches.

B How the text is organised

These sentences summarise the main idea of each paragraph. Match each sentence to the correct paragraph.
   a) British managers change jobs within a company far more often than the Germans.
   b) A study has shown big differences in managerial behaviour in Britain and Germany. *paragraph 1*
   c) Approaches to management in both countries have disadvantages which are clearly different.
   d) British managers are 'generalists' rather than 'specialists'.
   e) Attitudes to the qualifications and the role of managers are different in Britain and Germany.
   f) The structure of British companies changes frequently.
   g) German managers are 'experts' in their jobs.

Management attitudes in Germany and Britain

Christopher Lorenz looks at the contrasting attitudes between German and British managers

Styles of execution

"MY GERMAN COUNTERPART KNOWS HOW TO CHANGE THE PLUG ON HIS EXECUTIVE TOY."

A study comparing British and German approaches to management has revealed the deep gulf which separates managerial behaviour in many German and British companies. The gap is so fundamental, especially among middle managers, that it can pose severe problems for companies from the two countries which either merge or collaborate. The findings are from a study called 'Managing in Britain and Germany' carried out by a team of German and British academics from Mannheim University and Templeton College, Oxford.

The differences are shown most clearly in the contrasting attitudes of many Germans and Britons to managerial expertise and authority, according to the academics. This schism results, in turn, from the very different levels of qualification, and sorts of career paths, which are typical in the two countries.

German managers – both top and middle – consider technical skill to be the most important aspect of their jobs, according to the study. It adds that German managers consider they earn their authority with colleagues and subordinates from this 'expert knowledge' rather than from their position in the organisational hierarchy.

In sharp contrast, British middle managers see themselves as executives first and technicians second. As a result, German middle managers may find that the only people within their British partner companies who are capable of helping them solve routine problems are technical specialists who do not have management rank. Such an approach is bound to raise status problems in due course.

Other practical results of these differences include a greater tendency of British middle managers to regard the design of their departments as their own responsibility, and to reorganise them more frequently than happens in Germany. German middle managers can have 'major problems in dealing with this', the academics point out, since British middle managers also change their jobs more often. As a result, UK organisations often undergo 'more or less constant change'.

Of the thirty British middle managers in the study, thirteen had held their current job for less than two years, compared with only three in Germany. Many of the Britons had also moved between unrelated departments or functional areas, for example from marketing to human resources. In contrast, all but one of the Germans had stayed in the same functional area. Twenty of them had occupied their current positions for five years or more, compared with only five of the Britons.

The researchers almost certainly exaggerate the strengths of the German pattern; its very stability helps to create the rigid attitudes which stop many German companies from adjusting to external change. But the authors of the report are correct about the drawbacks of the more unstable and less technically oriented British pattern. And they are right in concluding that the two countries do not merely have different career systems but also, in effect, different ways of doing business.

FINANCIAL TIMES
World business newspaper.

Management attitudes in Germany and Britain

Vocabulary tasks

A Words with similar or related meanings

1. The article mentions the 'gulf' (line 5) which separates managerial behaviour in German and British companies.
   a) Does the word 'gulf' suggest a big or small difference?
   b) Find two other words in the first two paragraphs of the article similar in meaning to 'gulf'.
2. The study is mainly concerned with middle managers. What words can be used to describe managers at levels above and below middle management. One example is in the text.
3. The article mentions that thirteen British managers 'had held their current job for less than two years' (line 82).
   a) What word could replace 'current'?
   b) Think of two other words with the same meaning as 'job'. One is in the article.
4. Many of the British managers had also moved between unrelated 'departments' or 'functional areas'. Two examples are given in the text (line 89). Can you think of at least four other 'functional areas' in a typical company?

B Collocations

1. Find at least three adjective–noun collocations in the text which create a negative impression (e.g. *severe problems*).
2. Match these verbs and nouns as they occur together in the text.
   a) pose   change
   b) carry out   problems
   c) solve   jobs
   d) undergo   a position
   e) change   a study
   f) occupy   problems

Sorry Hans, that's the boardroom this week, not the toilet! They've reorganised again!

C Word search

Find a word or phrase from the text that has a similar meaning.

1. work closely with another company (para 1)
   c..*ollaborate*..
2. skill of being a manager (para 2)
   m................ e....................
3. sequence of jobs you take during your working life (para 2)
   c.................... p....................
4. structure of an organisation with its different levels (para 3)
   o.................... h....................
5. companies that you are working closely with (para 4)
   p.................... c....................
6. problems which are not complex or difficult (para 4)
   r.................... p....................
7. position of being a manager (para 4)
   m.................... r....................

D Word families

Complete the chart.

verb	adjective	noun
manage	managerial	manager
manage	management	management
1 ....*Know*....	knowledgeable	2 ....
organise	3	4 ....
5	6	adjustment
7	8	collaborator

Over to you

1. From what you have read and heard, do you agree with the points made in the text?
2. If you have experience of working with managers from countries such as Japan, Sweden, USA or France, how would you describe their approach to management and organisation?
3. If you were going to collaborate with a British or German company, what could the potential problems be?
4. Write a short report giving suggestions and recommendations on ways to try to avoid or reduce these problems.

UNIT 10 The value of MBAs

Before you read

Discuss these questions.
1 What do the letters MBA stand for?
2 In your country how important is it to have an MBA to succeed in management?
3 Do you know many people who have an MBA, or who are studying or plan to study for one? Are you one of them? What are the reasons for doing so?

Reading tasks

A Understanding main points

Read the text on the opposite page about different attitudes towards MBA graduates and answer these questions.
1 What is the attitude of UK employers to MBAs? Are they very positive, negative or in between?
2 Several top business schools are mentioned in the text – which ones are they? Do you agree with this list? Would you add others?
3 According to the article, do most MBA students pay for themselves?
4 In which country are MBAs very highly regarded by employers, according to the article?

B Understanding details

1 Four companies are mentioned in the article. Rank them in order in terms of their attitude to MBAs, starting with the one most in favour.
2 Some disadvantages about MBAs are mentioned by people quoted in the article. What are they?
3 Businesses are generally grouped into two broad categories – manufacturing and production on one side, and services on the other side. Into which categories do the four companies mentioned in the article fit? What does this tell you about the type of companies which generally favour MBAs? Is this the case in your country too?

C How the text is organised

The article has four main parts, each one describing the attitude of one company to MBAs. Each part has a clear introductory sentence that indicates whether the company is in favour of MBAs or not. Find the introductory sentences and decide if the sentence indicates a positive or negative attitude to MBAs.

None more so than top management consulting firm Mckinsey. (positive)

What do employers say?

Getting an MBA is one thing. Getting employers to take it seriously is another. MBAs have not traditionally commanded the same respect in the UK as in the US, but an increasing number of UK employers are now taking them very seriously indeed.

None more so than top management consulting firm McKinsey. Of its 260 London consultants, around half have MBAs. The company actively recruits 30–40 people a year from major business schools, such as INSEAD in France, Harvard and Stanford in the US, and London Business School and Manchester in the UK. It spends around £1 million a year sponsoring its 25–30 graduate recruits to complete full-time MBAs at the same institutions.

'Essentially we see an MBA as a short cut to business experience', says Julian Seaward, head of recruitment for McKinsey's London Office. 'It enriches people with a lot of management theory, and perhaps a bit of jargon thrown in.'

However, the company still prefers MBAs gained abroad. With a longer established reputation in the US, business schools there still have the edge in attracting candidates, while INSEAD has positioned itself as an international school with a cosmopolitan faculty and student body.

'The networking and experience of other cultures is very useful as a lot of our clients are global', says Seaward.

Nevertheless, McKinsey is actively raising its profile over here with a recently-launched scheme offering external candidates sponsorship through a United Kingdom MBA with a guaranteed job afterwards.

With a £50,000 Harvard MBA, McKinsey knows how attractive its staff are to other employers. Those who wish to leave within two years have to repay their sponsorship, but Seaward believes the staff development strategy has a good return rate. 'We look for people to develop a long-term career with us, not just an analyst job for a couple of years, and reward high achievers with good salaries and opportunities.'

Equally convinced of the value of MBAs is direct marketing company OgilvyOne Worldwide, which recently established an MBA bursary for staff members.

Chairman Nigel Howlett believes the MBA's formal education in analytical skills and constructing solutions provides a very useful training, producing people who have a good overview of business issues rather than a concern for details.

The company is currently undertaking an evaluation of the best UK schools in which to invest their bursary. With the recent big increase in the number of institutions offering MBAs, Howlett is concerned that not all MBAs are equal. 'There are clear differences in terms of quality.'

But not every company favours MBAs. In the early 1990s, Shell actually abandoned its own MBA course at Henley when it realised it was not producing graduates who fitted the jobs for which they were destined.

'We're slightly ambivalent towards MBAs,' says Andy Gibb, Shell's head of global recruitment. 'A lot of Shell's work is technical, while MBAs from leading schools are pitched at a more strategic level. It can be frustrating and unnecessary to be trained for strategic thinking, when the job you're moving into is not really suited to that. We would rather focus them on technical leadership.'

Companies like chartered accountants PricewaterhouseCoopers take a more middle-of-the-road approach. While it does not actively target MBAs or recruit them directly from business schools, a growing proportion of its senior consultants have got them, and it is increasingly on the lookout for MBA graduates.

'Our business is changing from audit and tax management more into consultancy roles,' says UK recruitment partner Keith Bell. 'MBAs do bring a breadth of vision to the business problem rather than a narrow viewpoint, and that can be an advantage. But the issue is the longer term. If you sponsor someone to do an MBA, will you get them back again?'

From *The Independent*

The value of MBAs

Vocabulary tasks

A Word search

Find a word or phrase from the text that has a similar meaning.

1 select and employ new people in a company (para 2)
   r. *ecruit*
2 give financial support to a student (para 2)
   s....................
3 special vocabulary of a field of work (para 3)
   j....................
4 making useful contacts with lots of people (para 5)
   n....................
5 people who are ambitious to succeed in their job (para 7)
   h.................... a....................
6 neither for nor against something (para 12)
   a....................

B Collocations

Match the verbs and nouns as they occur together in the text.

1 command   a) a profile
2 be   b) an evaluation
3 have   c) a middle-of-the-road approach
4 raise   d) respect
5 undertake   e) the edge
6 establish   f) a career
7 take   g) a reputation
8 develop   h) on the look out

C Complete the sentence

Use an appropriate phrase from Exercise B to complete each sentence.

1 We are always ....*on the lookout*........ for talented people to join our creative team.
2 The success of its advertising campaign helped the business school .... among international companies.
3 Because of our continued investment in research we .... over many of our competitors.
4 To help us choose which business school to work with we will need to .... of the top ten.
5 Studying for an MBA is increasingly necessary as a way to .... in a large organisation.

D Linking

Find at least four examples in the article where a contrast is made. Note the word or phrase used to introduce the contrast, and say what is being contrasted, e.g. <u>However</u>, *the company still prefers MBAs gained abroad* (line 20) – contrast between MBAs from abroad and MBAs from UK business schools.

Over to you

1 Should companies have some of the following policies towards MBAs?
   - sponsor students fully and with no conditions
   - sponsor students partly and/or with conditions
   - form a partnership with a particular business school to design a 'company-specific' MBA
   - recruit only from the top international business schools

2 Many people study for MBAs part-time over several years, or even by distance learning. What are the advantages and disadvantages of this route compared to a full-time MBA? Which route would you prefer?

3 Imagine that you are applying to a business school to do an MBA. Write a letter of application giving brief details of your work experience and previous education. Also give some reasons why you want to study for an MBA.

UNIT 11 Recruiting internationally

Before you read

Discuss these questions.
1 What are the most popular subjects to study at universities and colleges in your country? Why?
2 If you wanted to find out about job opportunities or vacancies at a large company or international organisation, how would you do it?

Reading tasks

A Understanding main points

1 Which of these statements gives the best summary of the text on the opposite page?
   a) A global company needs to recruit globally.
   b) The Internet will revolutionise the way new employees are recruited.
   c) Engineering is the discipline of the future.

2 Mark these statements T (true) or F (false) according to the information in the text. Find the part of the text that gives the correct information.
   a) DaimlerChrysler is the largest employer in Baden-Wurttemburg. F
   b) Daimler Chrysler employs more people in Baden-Wurttemburg than in other parts of Germany.
   c) The company plans to increase its investment in research and development.
   d) DaimlerChryslers' policy is to recruit engineers in Germany whenever possible.
   e) DaimlerChrysler uses the Internet in its recruitment campaigns.
   f) BMW is a more attractive company to work for.
   g) Not enough students study engineering in Germany.
   h) DaimlerChrysler is planning to set up its own technical university.

B How the text is organised

These phrases summarise the main idea of each paragraph. Match each phrase with the correct paragraph.
   a) the need to recruit engineers globally to meet it's business targets
   b) the lack of engineering graduates generally
   c) DaimlerChrysler's position in the state of Baden-Wurttemburg   paragraph 1
   d) the need to compete with other companies to attract new recruits
   e) DaimlerChrysler's business targets
   f) use of the Internet for recruitment
   g) DaimlerChrysler's plans to support private universities
   h) another recruitment approach

Recruiting internationally

DAIMLERCHRYSLER: Star is reminder of proud auto heritage by **Jeremy Grant**

Where have all the engineers gone?

For the past year Daimler has been part of the grouping with American manufacturer Chrysler. The German company's roots go back to the very first days of motoring.

If Germans associate one company with the state of Baden-Wurttemberg it is the automotive group DaimlerChrysler. The group was formed in 1998 through the merger of Daimler-Benz and Chrysler of the US. But the local association dates back to the late 1890s, when Daimler and Benz began the automotive age by producing the world's first motor cars. DaimlerChrysler is one of the mainstays of the Baden-Wurttemberg economy, sustaining 242,000 people in employment across Germany – the bulk of them in the state.

To extend its global reach, the company has ambitious plans to grow in the automotive business, and will invest €46bn developing sixty-four new cars and truck models in the next few years. Research and development spending is set to soar to what a spokesman says is 'a market leading position'. This year the company aims for sales of €146bn, compared with previous forecasts of €139.9bn.

One of the most critical issues facing the group as it attempts to achieve those targets is where it will find, in sufficient numbers, people with the right qualifications to make it all happen. Baden-Wurttemberg and Germany alone will not be able to provide enough recruits. 'DaimlerChrysler needs to hire 4,500 engineers and IT people in the next three years,' says Marc Binder of Human Resources. 'That's a big number and it will be impossible to find enough of them in Germany, let alone in one region. You have to hire them from the top schools in the world.'

Traditionally, Daimler-Benz always recruited engineers within Germany. In 1999, however, its recruitment campaign went global. Part of the impetus was that the transatlantic merger had broadened the spectrum of job opportunities. Using the Internet, DaimlerChrysler issued a blanket invitation to college graduates around the world – with emphasis on mechanical engineering, process technology and aerospace engineering – to attend an open day at eleven DaimlerChrysler locations around the world. Of the 800 who attended, about 55 per cent were invited for interview – a far higher proportion than in previous recruitment drives.

A few months later, the group launched a novel campaign to attract recruits for its International Management Associate Program. It advertised in the international press, inviting would-be trainees to call a company hotline during a four-hour period over two days. Some 200 applicants were interviewed.

Competition for talent from other large industrial groups is bound to increase. Rivals such as BMW, in neighbouring Bavaria, have similar needs. But Mr Binder says: 'We try to convince would-be recruits that we're the most global company and it's more interesting to work at DaimlerChrysler in this exciting period after the merger.' Recruits are also offered opportunities to work in different units of the group.

The recruitment problem has been made worse by a steady decline in the number of students electing to study engineering since the early 1990s – when there were too many newly-qualified engineers entering the market. Large numbers of students chose to study other subjects, leading to today's shortage.

DaimlerChrysler is supporting initiatives to try to ensure a steady flow of engineers and graduates from other technical disciplines. Over the course of the next few years, the group will be supporting the establishment of two private universities in Baden-Wurttemberg – the Stuttgart Institute of Management and Technology and the International University of Germany in Bruchsal.

FINANCIAL TIMES
World business newspaper.

DAIMLERCHRYSLER

Recruiting internationally

Vocabulary tasks

A Synonyms

1. The writer uses three different words to describe an institute of higher education. What are they? Are they exact equivalents?
2. Two words are used many times with the meaning of 'to find and employ new people'. What are they?
3. The word 'campaign' is used twice in the article (lines 50 and 68). What other phrase is used with a similar meaning to 'campaign'?
4. 'about 55 per cent of graduates who attended DaimlerChrysler's open day were invited for interview' (line 63).
   a) What other word is used in the article with a similar meaning to 'about'?
   b) Think of at least three other words or phrases to give the idea of approximation.

B Word search

1. The article deals mainly with the theme of recruitment. Find at least ten words or phrases in the text connected with the idea of recruitment
2. The writer uses several phrases to express the idea of time, either as an approximate date, e.g. 'the late 1890s' (line 8) or to describe when something will or did happen, e.g. 'in the next few years' (line 23). How many similar time expressions can you find in the article?

C Complete the sentence

Use an appropriate word or phrase from Exercise A or B to complete each sentence.

1. Due to rapid expansion the company had to carry out an extensive ..*recruitment campaign*.. to hire new employees.
2. In .... very few people knew much about the Internet.
3. .... the next few years the use of the Internet is bound to expand even more.
4. There are literally hundreds of business .... around the world offering MBAs.
5. Many companies now .... new job vacancies on the Internet and in the press simultaneously.
6. .... graduates in subjects such as information technology have a lot of opportunities for their first job.
7. Our recruitment campaign was so successful that we had over 100 .... for each job.
8. We usually invite about 5 per cent of those who apply to come for ...., so we can meet them in person.
9. An MBA is one of the best .... for an international management job.

D Expanding vocabulary

1. The article focuses on the subject of engineering. There are many different branches of engineering. Two are mentioned in the article – mechanical engineering and aerospace engineering (line 58). What other branches of engineering can you think of?

2. The article mentions that there is a 'steady decline' in the numbers of engineering students, leading to a 'shortage' of potential recruits (line 91).
   a) Think of at least two other words similar in meaning to 'decline'.
   b) Think of at least three words with the opposite meaning.
   c) Think of at least one word equivalent in meaning to 'shortage'.
   d) Think of at least one word with the opposite meaning.

E Definitions

Match these terms with their definitions.

1. mainstay (line 13)
2. global reach (line 18)
3. set to soar (line 24)
4. impetus (line 51)
5. broadened the spectrum of job opportunities (line 52)
6. blanket invitation (line 55)
7. a novel campaign (line 68)
8. would-be trainees (line 73)

a) an influence that makes something happen
b) people who want to enter a training programme
c) a new and imaginative way to recruit
d) having a presence all over the world
e) an offer open to everyone
f) about to increase a lot
g) increased the range of possible jobs
h) most important part of something

Over to you

1. Imagine you work in the Human Resources department of a large international company such as DaimlerChrysler. You are attending a recruitment fair at a major university. Prepare and give a presentation about the company and the career prospects for university graduates.

2. You have seen a list of jobs advertised on the Internet by an international manufacturing company – they want to recruit people for technical, commercial and administrative positions. Write a letter of application, specifying which kind of vacancy you are interested in and mentioning your relevant qualifications and experience.

3. Look at the websites of some well-known international companies. Describe their approach to recruitment using the Internet.

UNIT 12 Selecting international managers

Before you read

Discuss these questions.

1 What are the different methods a company can use to find new employees? Which are you most familiar with? Which do you think are most effective?
2 What are the most common selection methods used by companies and organisations in your country, (e.g. interviews, intelligence tests)? Do you think selection methods vary from country to country?

Reading tasks

A Understanding main points

Mark these statements T (true) or F (false) according to the information in the text on the opposite page. Find the part of the text that gives the correct information.

1 Many international organisations have decentralised selection. T
2 They look for different personal qualities in different cultures.
3 The 'SWAN' criteria have international validity.
4 The definition of some qualities can lead to cultural misunderstandings.
5 Mobility and language capability are clearly understood across cultures.

B Understanding details

The text states that different cultures look for different qualities when selecting personnel. Match the cultures with the qualities or attributes according to the text.

1 Anglo-Saxon (UK, USA, Australia etc.)   c, f
2 Germanic
3 Latin
4 Far Eastern

a) being able to fit in with the organisation
b) having the relevant kind of education for the job
c) having the right intellectual or technical capabilities
d) having good interpersonal skills
e) having attended the 'top' universities in the country
f) being able to carry out relevant tasks and jobs

C Word search

Find at least five methods for testing or assessing a candidate's suitability for a job (e.g. *assessment centres*) which are mentioned in the text.

Recruitment and Selection

Approaches to selection vary significantly across cultures. There are differences not only in the priorities that are given to technical or interpersonal capabilities, but also in the ways that candidates are tested and interviewed for the desired qualities.

In Anglo-Saxon cultures, what is generally tested is how much the individual can contribute to the tasks of the organisation. In these cultures, assessment centres, intelligence tests and measurements of competencies are the norm. In Germanic cultures, the emphasis is more on the quality of education in a specialist function. The recruitment process in Latin and Far Eastern cultures is very often characterised by ascertaining how well that person 'fits in' with the larger group. This is determined in part by the elitism of higher educational institutions, such as the 'grandes ecoles' in France or the University of Tokyo in Japan, and in part by their interpersonal style and ability to network internally. If there are tests in Latin cultures, they will tend to be more about personality, communication and social skills than about the Anglo-Saxon notion of 'intelligence'.

Though there are few statistical comparisons of selection practices used across cultures, one recent study provides a useful example of the impact of culture. A survey conducted by Shackleton and Newell compared selection methods between France and the UK. They found that there was a striking contrast in the number of interviews used in the selection process, with France resorting to more than one interview much more frequently. They also found that in the UK there was a much greater tendency to use panel interviews than in France, where one-to-one interviews are the norm. In addition, while almost 74 per cent of companies in the UK use references from previous employers, only 11 per cent of the companies surveyed in France used them. Furthermore, French companies rely much more on personality tests and handwriting analysis than their British counterparts.

Many organisations operating across cultures have tended to decentralise selection in order to allow for local differences in testing and for language differences, while providing a set of personal qualities or characteristics they consider important for candidates.

Hewitt Associates, a US compensation and benefits consulting firm based in the Mid West, has had difficulties extending its key selection criteria outside the USA. It is known for selecting 'SWANs': people who are Smart, Willing, Able and Nice. These concepts, all perfectly understandable to other Americans, can have very different meanings in other cultures. For example, being able may mean being highly connected with colleagues, being sociable or being able to command respect from a hierarchy of subordinates, whereas the intended meaning is more about being technically competent, polite and relatively formal. Similarly, what is nice in one culture may be considered naive or immature in another. It all depends on the cultural context.

Some international companies, like Shell, Toyota, and L'Oréal, have identified very specific qualities that they consider strategically important and that support their business requirements. For example, the criteria that Shell has identified as most important in supporting its strategy include mobility and language capability. These are more easily understood across cultures because people are either willing to relocate or not. There is less room for cultural misunderstandings with such qualities.

From *Managing Cultural Differences*, Economist Intelligence Unit

Selecting international managers

Vocabulary tasks

A Synonyms

1 The word 'selection' is combined with a number of other words, all with similar meanings (e.g. *approaches to selection*). Find four other combinations starting with 'selection'.

2 The word 'skill' is often used in connection with job performance. It can be defined as 'the ability to do something well, especially because you have learned and practised it'. In the text, several other words are used with a similar meaning. What are they?

3 The acronym SWANs (line 77) stands for 'people who are *Smart, Willing, Able* and *Nice*'. Depending on the context, these words can have different meanings. Match each word with one of the SWAN words.

a) charming *nice*
b) helpful
c) clever
d) friendly
e) sociable
f) competent
g) enthusiastic
h) enjoyable
i) well-dressed
j) pleasant
k) eager
l) intelligent
m) beautiful
n) neat
o) kind
p) skilful

4 Which words from the list have exactly the same meaning as the SWAN words in the text?

B Linking

Use an appropriate word or phrase from the box to complete each sentence.

| for example   though   whereas   in addition   similarly |

1 The Internet is changing the way that companies work; *for example*, some use their website to advertise job vacancies.

2 Some companies use newspaper advertisements in the recruitment process, ... others prefer to use consultants.

3 With the boom in hi-tech industries, well-qualified software specialists are difficult to find; ...., in the automotive industry, there is a shortage of engineering graduates.

4 To get good management jobs, an MBA is now often a requirement; ...., knowledge of two foreign languages including English is increasingly demanded.

5 The Internet is being used more and more as a recruitment tool, ... there are few statistics available yet about how successful it is.

Selecting international managers

C Definitions

Match these terms with their definitions.

1. assessment (line 13)
2. the norm (line 16)
3. ascertaining (line 22)
4. elitism (line 24)
5. striking (line 44)
6. compensation and benefits (line 72)

a) finding out
b) noticeable
c) pay and conditions
d) evaluation
e) usual, standard
f) concern for status

Over to you

1. Make a list of qualities or skills that you think an international manager should have. Divide your list into technical skills and interpersonal skills.
2. What are the best ways to measure or evaluate technical skills?
3. How can you measure interpersonal skills?
4. Look at the chart showing selection methods in different countries.

Percentage use of selection methods in six different countries

Method of selection	UK	France	Germany	Israel	Norway	Netherlands	All
Interviews	92	97	95	84	93	93	93
References/recommendations	74	39	23	30	–	49	43
Cognitive tests	11	33	21	–	25	21	22
Personality tests	13	38	6	–	16	–	18
Graphology	3	52	–	2	2	24	13
Work sample	18	16	13	–	13	5	13
Assessment centres	14	8	10	3	10	–	8
Biodata	4	1	8	1	8	–	4
Astrology	–	6	–	1	–	–	2

Source: Robertson and Makin (1993)

Imagine you are an HR specialist in an international company. Use this information to make a presentation about selection methods the company should use in Northern Europe.

UNIT 13 Training across cultures

Before you read

Discuss these questions.
1 How do you most like to learn, e.g. lectures, discussions, multimedia, case studies?
2 Do you think there are different ways of learning and teaching in different countries? Can you think of some examples?

Reading tasks

A Understanding main points

1 Which of these statements gives the best summary of the text on the opposite page?
   a) Multinational companies should try to standardise their approach to training and development.
   b) The way people learn should be considered when planning international training courses.
   c) The US approach to training is the most effective.
2 Which approach to training in international organisations do you think the authors prefer?
   a) standardised training methods
   b) a mixed pedagogical approach

B Understanding details

Mark these statements T (true) or F (false) according to the information in the text. Find the part of the text that gives the correct information.
1 German and Swiss managers like training courses to be clear and well-structured. T
2 British managers dislike training courses and prefer to learn by doing things on the job.
3 Asian managers want to learn from the teacher, not from each other.
4 Courses attended by British and US participants often lead to conflict and arguments.
5 British trainers are often concerned about the status of participants in their seminars.
6 British and American trainers like using role plays and simulations.
7 European managers consider American training courses to be badly organised.

How to learn

Cultural differences are an important factor when it comes to how and what managers should learn and from whom. Different cultural responses to management education are particularly revealing. For example, German and Swiss managers tend to favour structured learning situations with clear pedagogical objectives, detailed course outlines and schedules, and the 'right answer' or superior solution. This is very much in contrast with the view typically held by people from Anglo-Saxon cultures such as Britain and the USA. Most British participants in courses dislike a structure that is too rigid. They tend to prefer more open-ended learning situations with loose objectives and practical tasks. The suggestion that there could be only one correct answer is less acceptable to them.

The idea of working in groups may come more naturally to Asian managers than to the more individualistic Anglo-Saxons. On the other hand, Asian participants experience more difficulty having to 'sell' their ideas in a group, with the potential for open disagreement and conflict, and therefore possible loss of face. Nor do they quite see the point of learning from other students who are no more knowledgeable than themselves. Wisdom resides in the hierarchy.

Group discussions may seem perfectly natural to Americans, who have been encouraged as students to express their own ideas and opinions. British students too have been educated to challenge and debate the ideas put forth by each other, including the teacher. British culture values the ability to prove one's case, eloquently, even at the expense of others. Anglo-Saxon culture is more tolerant of confrontation and uncertainty, and is less concerned with status differences, either among participants or between themselves and the teacher. This can be quite a shock to students from Asia and many Central European countries, who are not used to either voicing their opinion in class, disagreeing with each other, or actively debating with the professor.

Training that makes extensive use of case studies, business games, and management exercises such as role-plays, favours learning by doing rather than learning by lecture and reading. It indicates a preference for experiential or active learning rather than cognitive or reflective learning. It also reflects an inductive rather than deductive approach; cases or exercises are used to arrive at general principles or theories (the Anglo-Saxon approach) rather than starting with a theory or framework, which is then applied to a given situation (the approach in many countries in Europe). As a result, European managers may not always see the point of some of these exercises, and some complain that seminars conducted by US trainers are not sufficiently serious or theoretical. US managers, on the other hand, want training to be more concrete, practical and fun.

With each culture favouring different training and development practices, it may be difficult to integrate these into a coherent or consistent policy within an international organisation. However, standardising training methods may be important if the company needs to communicate specialised knowledge quickly across different units, or if the special quality of the company training programmes is regarded as a major source of attracting new recruits.

On the other hand, multinational companies may have a lot to gain from cross-fertilising different approaches, and providing opportunities for training and development that appeal to people with different abilities, learning styles, educational backgrounds, and, of course, cultures. In fact, working with groups of managers from different countries often requires a mixed pedagogical approach, as well as the use of trainers of different nationalities.

From *Managing Across Cultures*, Pearson Education Limited

C Understanding meanings

1 Choose the best explanation for the phrase 'loss of face' (line 34).
   a) when someone is embarrassed in front of others
   b) when someone has a different opinion from others in a discussion

2 Choose the best explanation for the phrase 'wisdom resides in the hierarchy' (line 37).
   a) older and more senior people have more knowledge than younger people
   b) you should never disagree with a teacher in public

Training across cultures

3 Match the approaches to teaching and learning from the box with their definitions.

| cognitive   experiential   inductive   deductive |

a) learning which involves reading, thinking about and understanding the main ideas of an issue   *cognitive*

b) studying the general rule in a theoretical way and then applying this to particular cases; in other words, going from the general to the particular

c) learning which involves taking part in activities and then discussing the results of the activity

d) looking at particular examples or cases and working out the general rule or principle which they demonstrate; in other words, going from the particular to the general

D How the text is organised

The following phrases summarise the purpose of each paragraph. Match each phrase with the correct paragraph.

a) cultures in which discussion and debate are favoured ways of learning

b) the importance of culture when planning the way training is structured   *paragraph 1*

c) the benefits of using different training styles

d) an intellectual and rational approach vs. a practical and activity-based approach

e) reasons for standardising training approaches

f) when group work can cause problems

Vocabulary tasks

A Contrast and comparison

1 The text uses the phrase 'in contrast with' (line 13) to express contrast. Find another phrase with a similar meaning.

2 In paragraph 4 the Anglo-Saxon and continental European approaches to teaching and learning are described and compared in considerable detail. One phrase is used four times to indicate the idea of preferring one way to another.

a) What is it?

b) Can you think of another phrase to replace it?

B Opposites

Find a word in the text that has an opposite meaning.

1 structured (line 8)   *open-ended*

2 clear (line 9)

3 reflective (line 70)

4 theoretical (line 85)

C Synonyms

Find a word in the text that has a similar meaning.

1 right (line 12)   *correct*
2 disagreement (line 32)
3 express ideas and opinions (line 42)
4 challenge (line 44)
5 development (line 108)

D Word search

Find a word or phrase from the text that has a similar meaning.

1 generally prefer (para 1)
   t..*end*............ to f..*avour*.........
2 something that is easier and more acceptable to do (para 2)
   c................... m.................... n...................
3 understand and accept an idea (para 2)
   s................... the p....................
4 absolutely normal or usual (para 3)
   p.................... n....................
5 to another person's disadvantage or embarrassment (para 3)
   at the e................... of o...................
6 worried about something (para 3)
   c...................
7 get great benefit from (para 6)
   h................... a l................... to g...................

Over to you

1 Do you agree with the authors' description of how different cultures like to learn?

2 A large US multinational, with subsidiaries all over the world, including many parts of Europe and Asia, has decided to run the same seminar for all its managers worldwide on the theme of 'cultural diversity'. The intention is that all employees should respect differences of race, culture and gender in the workplace. The company has commissioned a US training consultancy to run all these seminars. They will all be run in English, with the same course content. The same US trainers will run the seminars using a lot of activities such as role-plays and simulations.

How do you think this will work in practice when the course is run in different countries around the world? If you were going to attend the course in your country, what would your expectations be?

UNIT 14 International management development

Before you read

Discuss these questions.
1 What do you think would be the best ways to learn to be an international manager?
2 What do you know about management development in different countries? Is it very different?

Reading tasks

A Understanding main points
1 The text on the opposite page describes two international management development programmes, each designed for small groups of companies.
   a) How many companies take part in each programme?
   b) Which company is involved in both programmes?
2 What is the main emphasis on the London Business School (LBS) Programme?
   a) to learn about how different global businesses operate
   b) for the participants to learn from each other
   c) to provide experience of working in multinational teams
3 In which country does the second programme take place, and what language is used?

B Understanding details
1 Mark these statements T (true) or F (false) according to the information about the LBS Programme. Find the part of the text that gives the correct information.
   a) Much of the course is based on lectures and discussions. F
   b) The programme runs every year.
   c) The programme is aimed at young managers with high potential.
   d) The participants travel a lot as part of the programme.
   e) Part of the course involves staying in Brazil to get work experience.
   f) Each participant visits five different companies.
   g) The programme involves a lot of project work.
2 Which regions of the world are studied in the London Business School Programme and which important part of the world, from an economic point of view, seems not to be included?
3 Which of the two programmes offers a formal qualification, and what is it?
4 What are the characteristics of the course at Ashridge, as described in the article?
5 What are the characteristics of equivalent courses in Germany?

• YOU AND YOUR WORK

How to learn in a global classroom

Today's Tuesday, this must be Hong Kong. No, not the confused words of a jet-lagged traveller, but the words of an international executive on a business management course.

Our German manager from Lufthansa will have flown in to the former British colony on whistle-stop tours of LG, the Korean conglomerate, and Standard Chartered Bank, whose main operations are in the Middle East and Asia-Pacific, as part of his international training programme. After that, the next stop could be Brazil to see how ABB, the international engineering group, adapts its working practices to local conditions.

The globe-trotting executive is already a well-established figure in the international picture. But he or she is now being joined by the global executive on a management training course. Why hold dry in-house study programmes, repeating old ideas, when the environment that today's top-flight executives operate in is global? Business schools have responded by offering courses in which the international element is the central point. At London Business School's Global Business Consortium, for example, a senior manager from each of ABB, British Telecom, LG, Lufthansa, SKF from Sweden, and Standard Chartered Bank come together each year to learn about how different global businesses operate.

Each of the regions of Europe, Asia and South America are represented in the operations of these six blue chip multinationals. The emphasis is on participants learning from each other. Insights into cultural pitfalls and practical guidance are also part of the package.

But the only way of getting a feel for the special considerations of operating on the ground in another country is to visit the region itself and meet local leaders, academics and senior managers. Here course participants will aim to gain a better understanding of the relationship between global strategy and regional characteristics. Each of the participating companies acts as host to the other five as part of the module-based learning programme. On site they will work in a multinational team analysing various aspects of the host company's strategy.

The Ashridge European Partnership MBA has been running since September 1998. Three German companies – Lufthansa, Deutsche Bank and Merck – have formed a consortium enabling employees to study for an MBA with Ashridge Management College, in the UK.

'The English learning atmosphere is different from that in Germany,' said Dr Peter Weicht, director of personnel and organisational development at Merck, the international chemical and pharmaceutical group. 'It is good for team-building, which will be very important between different cultures. In England there is a more relaxed relationship between lecturer and student.'

Dr Martin Moehrle, head of management development for Deutsche Bank, also favours global training. 'In Germany we are too domestically oriented; to become more international it is a must to be exposed to the English language and to other industries.'

He was impressed, too, by the 'modern approach' of the Ashridge MBA compared with its more technical, accounting-led German equivalent, which is less concerned with leadership issues.

Another plus for organisations favouring the international element in training is that it will help them to attract those ambitious men and women who want to continue their studies. These training options enable high-fliers to carry on with education without leaving the company.

However, there are drawbacks. Deutsche Bank, in particular, has had the experience of talented employees leaving their job to attend the Ashridge course, only to join another company later. ❑

From *The Independent on Sunday*

International management development

Vocabulary tasks

A Word search

1 The text describes two 'business management courses', which is a compound noun made up of three separate nouns. Find at least ten others in the text, either with two or three nouns.
2 The word 'course' is used a lot in the article. What other word is used with a similar meaning?
3 In the first three paragraphs there are several words and phrases used to describe aspects of travelling. Find a word or a phrase from the text that has a similar meaning.
   a) a person who feels tired from too much travelling
   b) a very quick visit to a place
   c) a person who travels around the world on business
4 Words associated with flying are used to describe people with talent and potential, especially in business. There are two examples in the text (paras 3 and 10). What are they? Do they have the same meaning?

International management development

B Understanding expressions

1 The London Business School's Global Business Consortium consists of six 'blue chip multinationals' (line 46). Choose the best explanation for the phrase 'blue chip'.

   a) large and very profitable
   b) well-established and well-known
   c) listed on the stock market

2 One of the six companies, the Korean group LG is described as a 'conglomerate' (line 10). Choose the best explanation for the word 'conglomerate'.

   a) a company operating in many different countries
   b) a large company with many subsidiaries
   c) a very large company which is in many different kinds of business

C Definitions

Match these terms with their definitions.

1 dry (line 27)
2 pitfalls (line 49)
3 getting a feel for (line 52)
4 operating on the ground (line 54)
5 a must (line 96)
6 another plus (line 105)
7 drawbacks (line 114)

a) something essential
b) serious and academic in style
c) dangers
d) understanding and experiencing
e) working in a real situation
f) an extra advantage
g) disadvantages

Over to you

1 The article describes two very different types of training programme – one very project orientated and the other more traditional, involving lectures, case studies, etc. Which do you think might be more effective for producing international managers? Which programme would you prefer to attend?

2 Do you think the two approaches to management development are suited to different kinds of people, in terms of age, experience, cultural background, education, the industry they work in? If so, why?

3 Imagine you work in the management development department of one of the six multinationals which take part in the London Business School programme. Write a description of the programme, asking for applications from managers in the company; this will be circulated on the company's intranet around the world.

UNIT 15 Thinking global, acting local

Before you read

Discuss these questions.
1 The phrase 'think global, act local' is often quoted. What does it mean to you?
2 A lot is said and written about 'global organisations'. What do you understand by this phrase? Which organisations are global, in your opinion? Why?

Reading tasks

A Understanding main points

1 Which of these statements gives the best summary of the text on the opposite page?
   a) Having expatriates in key positions is still important for international companies.
   b) Using local managers rather than expatriates is now the objective of most companies.
   c) Developing managers from around the world who share the company's values is essential for global success.

2 According to Lowell Bryan of McKinsey, how many international companies are not dominated by the culture of the home country – a lot, or just a few? What is the phrase he uses?

B Understanding details

Mark these statements T (true) or F (false) according to the information in the text.
Find the part of the text that gives the correct information.
1 Few companies are genuinely global. T
2 The use of expatriates is growing at Unilever.
3 Corporate culture is more important than local needs in most areas of management.
4 Recruiting local managers is difficult for many organisations.
5 It is important to offer a career path for local managers.
6 Unilever manages people differently in different countries.
7 Many multinationals impose their British, French, German or US approach to business on all their subsidiaries.
8 Unilever believes it is difficult to have a consistent measure of management potential worldwide.

C Understanding meanings

1 Richard Greenhalgh thinks a younger generation of managers is more likely to have travelled and taken MBAs abroad (lines 47–50). Choose the best explanation for the statement.
   a) they will be more ambitious and want higher salaries
   b) they will have a better understanding of business issues
   c) they will be more international in their attitudes

60

Perspective: The myth of the global executive

The key to success is to combine corporate culture with local knowledge and include, not reject national characteristics, writes Tony Jackson

Multinationals running their various businesses the same way all over the world may have been perfectly acceptable 30 years ago, but it is not the way today. Nevertheless, the vast majority of even the biggest companies still have a culture rooted in their country of origin. Changing that is one of the biggest challenges to becoming genuinely global.

Richard Greenhalgh, head of management development and training at the Anglo-Dutch consumer group Unilever, says that in a few areas, such as integrity and the Unilever code of conduct, corporate culture takes precedence.

'But you need a balance between having a very international cadre and having a national presence,' he says. 'A few years ago, we were concerned that we had too many expatriates. Five years ago, three of our four business heads in Italy were expatriates. Now they're all Italian. In a consumer business like ours, that's important.'

The global executive, in fact, may be something of a myth. According to Mr Greenhalgh, the use of expatriates goes against the policy of providing a career ladder for local managers.

In fact, however global the company may be, it remains necessary to manage people differently in different countries. Within Europe, Mr Greenhalgh says, Unilever has traditionally been much more open with managers in northern than southern countries, on matters such as where they stand in the salary scale or what their prospects are. But that is changing, he adds. A younger generation of managers is more likely to have travelled when young, and many have taken an MBA in the US.

Behind this lies the most fundamental problem of all: the fact that apart from a handful of companies, even the biggest corporations are dominated by the culture of the home country. 'Outside that handful,' says Lowell Bryan, a senior partner with McKinsey in New York, 'companies are very German, or very British, or very American. And in the case of US companies they assume globalisation means Americanising the world. At least others don't have that arrogance.'

But if the members of top management are all nationals of the home country, it makes it much more difficult to attract and keep talented and ambitious managers from other countries. In fact, the problem lies not in attracting people – a talented Indian or Korean manager will typically want early experience with a multinational – but in keeping them. 'People will join the company to learn,' Mr Bryan says, 'but unless they feel they're part of the core company, they're going to leave, and exploit the brand status of the company in their next job.'

So given the importance of local cultures within the global company, an obvious question is how to appraise and identify talent around the world on a consistent basis. Unilever, Mr Greenhalgh says, has been working on this for the past four years.

'We've been developing a set of eleven management competencies we can use worldwide', he says. 'The aim is to have a clear objective measure of potential. We measure such things as entrepreneurial drive, the ability to lead and develop others, and integrity. That makes up a common core of behaviours. We've tested it, and so far it seems to be culturally transferable.'

FINANCIAL TIMES
World business newspaper.

---

2 Lowell Bryan says that some local managers will leave and 'exploit the brand status of the company in their next job'. (line 80). What does this mean?

   a) they will take information about the company's products to a new company

   b) they will get a good job in a new company because of the reputation of their old company

   c) they will get good jobs as brand managers in a new company

3 Greenhalgh lists 'entrepreneurial drive' as one of eleven management competencies selected by Unilever (line 96). Choose the best explanation for the phrase.

   a) willingness to take risks in order to achieve goals

   b) previous experience of running a company

   c) someone with an outgoing personality

Thinking global, acting local

Vocabulary tasks

A Understanding expressions

Choose the best explanation for each of these words or phrases from the text.

1 code of conduct (line 18)
   a) rules of behaviour in business
   b) rules about use of company cars

2 international cadre (line 21)
   a) a special group of managers who work internationally
   b) a clear strategy for working internationally

3 career ladder (line 34)
   a) way of moving quickly to the top of the organisation
   b) way to make step-by-step progress in an organisation

4 salary scale (line 45)
   a) range of salaries related to particular jobs
   b) balance between salary and annual bonus

5 prospects (line 46)
   a) potential new clients
   b) future developments in your career

6 core company (line 79)
   a) the group of people at the heart of the company
   b) a special group of company consultants

7 appraise (line 86)
   a) congratulate people
   b) evaluate people's skills

B Complete the sentence

Use an appropriate word or phrase from Exercise A to complete each sentence.

1 Most ambitious young people want to join an organisation with a clear ...*career ladder*........., so they can see how their career will develop.

2 Socially responsible companies include business ethics in their ....

3 A graduate who joins a large international company will probably have better .... than one who joins a small family company.

4 The purpose of the annual meeting between a manager and his or her subordinates is to .... the subordinates' job performance.

5 Government organisations usually have a fixed ...., which links pay to job grades.

C Definitions

Match these terms with their definitions.

1. rooted in their country of origin (line 8)
2. takes precedence (line 19)
3. a myth (line 31)
4. more open with (line 41)
5. where they stand (line 44)
6. a handful of companies (line 53)
7. 'Americanising' the world (line 63)

a) something people believe but which is not true
b) to be strongly influenced by your home culture
c) to come first, to have priority
d) to turn everything into a copy of America
e) their position
f) a small number
g) give more information

D Word families

Complete the chart.

verb	adjective	noun
globalise	global	globalisation
appraise	1 *appraisal*	2 ....
3	consumer	4 ....
5	6	corporation
7	transferable	8 ....
9	10	success
identify	11	12 ....
13	14	measure

Over to you

1. The phrase *corporate culture* is used several times in the article. How would you define it? Give some examples of elements which make up the corporate culture of an organisation.

2. Greenhalgh says that 'Unilever has traditionally been much more open with managers in northern than southern countries' (line 40). What do you understand by this, and why do you think Unilever had this policy?

3. Unilever has developed a set of eleven management competencies, three of which are mentioned at the end of the article. If you had to choose one of these as the most important, which would it be and why? Discuss what other competencies a multinational such as Unilever might have in its list and try to produce a list of at least five others.

UNIT 16 Routes to top management

Before you read

Discuss these questions.
1 What kind of education offers the best route to top management positions in your country?
2 What kind of problems could you imagine in a joint venture between British and French companies, especially if one of them is from the private sector and another from the public or state sector.

Reading tasks

A Understanding main points

Read the text on the opposite page about a top French manager and answer these questions.
1 What business is Alstom in?
2 What is Pierre Bilger's position in the company?
3 Who owned Alcatel-Alsthom in the 1980s?
4 Is Alstom still a French–British company?

B Understanding details

Mark these statements T (true) or F (false) according to the information in the text. Find the part of the text that gives the correct information.
1 British and French business cultures have many things in common. F
2 The British tend to take decisions more quickly than the French.
3 The French do not like having long discussions to analyse things in detail.
4 The French feel they are systematic and logical in their approach to business.
5 British business people like to follow a strict agenda at meetings.
6 Alstom is no longer a purely French–British company.
7 In Alstom the French and English languages have equal status.
8 In Britain, manufacturing companies attract the best-qualified and cleverest people.

C Understanding details

Complete the chart showing the different stages of Bilger's education and career.

First higher education institution	a) *Institut des Etudes Politiques*
Second higher education institution	b)
First main employer	c)
Second main employer	d)
New name of company from 1988	e)
Current name of company	f)

Routes to top management

Industrialist honed by French polish

Like most of France's technocratic elite, Pierre Bilger is a Europhile and sees Alstom, the Anglo-French group he chairs, as an experiment in European unity

Few people better personify the French technocratic elite that has held France in a tight grip for many decades than Pierre Bilger. Bilger is the Chairman of Alstom, the giant power and railway equipment company formed out of the joint venture between Britain's General Electric Company (GEC) and France's Alcatel-Alsthom, which became a separately quoted company in 1998.

In his long career, Bilger has moved effortlessly from government to big business with the ease that the French state seems to encourage. He was born in 1940, in the Alsace region of eastern France. After school, he attended first the Institut des Etudes Politiques, then the prestigious Ecole Nationale d'Administration (ENA), the elite finishing school for French technocrats and many future government leaders.

On graduating, Bilger, like many of his ENA colleagues, joined the Finance Ministry, rising quickly up its ranks. In 1982 he switched from government to industry, joining CGE, as Alcatel-Alsthom was then known, although since the company was at that time owned by the French state, the change was more apparent than real.

At Alcatel-Alsthom his big project was overseeing the formation in 1988 of the joint venture with GEC. As soon as the joint venture, GEC-Alsthom, was formed, Bilger was given the task of running it.

After a decade of working for one of the largest Anglo-French joint ventures, Bilger is well attuned to Anglo-Saxon attitudes. He speaks frequently of shareholders and of the need to keep costs down but he still remains very French. His explanations are fluent and polished and his arguments have none of the down-to-earth style you might expect from someone running a British engineering company.

Although Britain and France are neighbours, their business cultures could hardly be further apart. What, I ask, had he found most irritating about the English once he was put in charge of a company full of them? 'What I found most irritating about our British colleagues was their great reluctance to go through what we French would consider a rational process of making a decision,' he answered thoughtfully. 'They insist on going straight to the point, whereas we like to have a systematic agenda. But over time I came to appreciate that this had its virtues as well.'

Like most French establishment figures, Bilger is an ardent Europhile. The company, he believes, is itself an experiment in unity; soon after the British and French parts were put together, German and Spanish units were added. After a brief attempt at using multiple languages inside the company, Bilger soon decided to impose English as the company language, partly because the English were reluctant to learn any other languages. 'We lost a few French managers because of that, but not many,' he says.

Alstom remains a technological leader and it is led by bright people. Bilger does not mention it, but in France the country's cleverest, best-qualified people can be found running manufacturing companies. In Britain that has not been true for almost a century.

From *The Sunday Times*

Routes to top management

Vocabulary tasks

A Collocations

Match these verbs and nouns as they occur together in the text.

1 go through
2 run
3 form
4 keep
5 make
6 give someone

a) a task
b) a process
c) a joint venture
d) a company
e) a decision
f) costs down

B Definitions

Match these terms with their definitions.

1 hold in a tight grip
2 technocratic elite
3 rise up its ranks
4 change was more apparent than real
5 attuned to
6 down-to-earth
7 could hardly be further apart
8 reluctant to
9 go straight to the point
10 have its virtues
11 an ardent Europhile
12 bright

a) discuss the most important things immediately
b) control something completely
c) are completely different
d) be very familiar with something, and to understand it well
e) very clever and intelligent
f) unsophisticated, not elegant or polished
g) have some advantages or good points
h) small group of people with a high level of technical education
i) be promoted in an organisation
j) someone who is very much in favour of a united Europe
k) be unhappy or unwilling to do something
l) there was no significant difference

C Complete the sentence

Use an appropriate word or phrase from Exercise A or B to complete each sentence.

1. In a recession, companies need to economise and *keep costs down* as much as possible.
2. We need to .... quickly before it is too late.
3. Many people are .... learn foreign languages because it takes a long time.
4. Each way of working ....; it's important not to criticise people just because they do something in a different way.
5. In the UK, business sectors such as advertising, the media, investment banking and management consultancy tend to attract .... people.
6. The most successful companies are .... the needs of their customers.
7. In many countries around the world, dictatorial leaders hold their country ....
8. He's a real high-flier who managed to .... to Managing Director in five years.
9. When a project is very big, two or more companies often .... in order to do the work.
10. In cultures where people like to avoid direct statements, they can be offended by people who .... in discussions.

D Expanding vocabulary

Notice the words *technocrat* and *Europhile* used to describe Pierre Bilger. What other words ending in –crat or –phile can you think of which fit the definitions below?

1. someone who works in a government organisation and follows official rules very strictly
2. someone similar to **1)** but who works for one of the EU institutions such as the European Commission
3. someone who likes England and the English
4. someone who likes France and the French

Over to you

1. The heads of many government ministries in France and the chief executives of many large state companies such as Renault, BNP and TotalFinaElf are nearly always graduates from ENA. They form a small technocratic elite who all know each other well. What do you think are the advantages and disadvantages of this? Is the situation similar in your country?

2. Bilger gives one example of differences in business culture between Britain and France: the French desire for a rational and logical approach to decision-making compared with the British preference for going straight to the point. What are the advantages and disadvantages of each approach?

3. Which approach is more similar to your business culture? Think of some examples.

UNIT 17 Overseas postings

Before you read

Discuss these questions.
1 What are the benefits and advantages to an executive and his or her family of working abroad for several years?
2 What are the possible disadvantages and dangers?

Reading tasks

A Understanding main points

1 Which of these statements gives the best summary of the text on the opposite page?
   a) Fewer young managers want to work abroad than in the past.
   b) Companies should prepare and support families in overseas postings.
   c) Most spouses of expatriates want to work when they are abroad.
2 According to the text, is an overseas posting becoming more or less popular for ambitious managers? Why?
3 Which company seems to be the most generous in its financial support for expatriate couples?
4 What is the main reason mentioned in the article for the failure of an overseas posting?
5 What are the consequences of failed postings?

B Understanding details

Mark these statements T (true) or F (false) according to the information in the text.
Find the part of the text that gives the correct information.
1 Companies send only the best candidates on overseas postings. F
2 Finding the right people for expatriate postings is difficult.
3 High-fliers are the people who most want to work overseas.
4 Shell prefers to give expatriates advice and information rather than money.
5 Most accompanying partners want to be able to work in the foreign country.
6 EBRD organises jobs for the spouses of its expatriates.

C Understanding meanings

1 Choose the best explanation for the sentence 'Companies ignore the problem of the "trailing spouse" at their peril' (line 1)?
   a) Some companies have never thought about this problem.
   b) It is very important for companies to try to deal with this problem.
   c) It is dangerous to send families to some parts of the world.

MANAGEMENT OVERSEAS POSTINGS

Don't forget the trailing spouse

Edi Smockum looks at some innovative solutions to the problems of working abroad

Companies ignore the problem of the 'trailing spouse' – those selfless individuals who follow their partners around the globe – at their peril. That was the warning, at a recent conference held in Paris, from Markus Andres, human resources manager for Zurich Insurance.

With the pool of potential employees who are willing to accept overseas postings shrinking, 'the remaining candidates may not represent the best possible selection,' he pointed out. A recent survey underlined the problem: 74 per cent of human resources managers said their chief global challenge was finding candidates. The most frequent reason for employees turning down expatriate appointments was concern about their spouse's career. If your company's high-flier is married to another high-flier with a different company, can you entice them to set off to foreign parts?

Some companies have found innovative solutions. Motorola, which has 2,000 expatriate employees worldwide, offers trailing spouses up to US$7,500 a year for education. This is broadly interpreted by the company – a spouse can, for example, use the money to invest in starting up a business. Shell International Petroleum, the Anglo-Dutch oil company which has 20 per cent of its employees serving in overseas appointments, reimburses 80 per cent of the costs of vocational training, further education or re-accreditation up to US$4,200 per assignment.

But, as Shell found, many potential expatriates are hungrier for information and advice than they are for funding. Its spouse employment centre has helped more than 1,000 couples prepare for placements overseas. The centre recommends schools, medical facilities and housing advice and provides up-to-date information on employment, study, self-employment and voluntary work. This support, fully funded by Shell, has been found to be very cost efficient.

Failed postings are a great risk in expatriate placements, and one that few companies take precautions against. Not only are the costs of returning a recently-moved employee and family high, it can damage relations with local clients. Family breakdown or maladjustment is the most cited reason for an employee to have to be repatriated.

Schlumberger, the French–US oil services company, extended its worldwide company intranet to include trailing spouses with home computers. This not only gave the accompanying partner access to Schlumberger's intranet, but also allowed them on to the world wide web.

But the main obstacle for most trailing spouses is the difficulty in getting a work permit. Many multilateral organisations, such as the London-based European Bank for Reconstruction and Development (EBRD), have been able to negotiate work permits for trailing spouses during the course of selecting sites for their offices.

Kathleen van der Wilk-Carlton of Shell thinks companies should begin to flex their muscles: 'If governments can get agreements for work permits for diplomatic staff, it is time for companies to lobby governments for the same rights.'

FINANCIAL TIMES
World business newspaper.

---

2 What is the best explanation for the phrase 'can you entice them [high-fliers] to set off for foreign parts?' (line 27)?
   a) Can you oblige them to go overseas without their spouse?
   b) Can you tell them to go overseas alone?
   c) Can you persuade them to go overseas with their spouse?

3 The way in which Motorola's offer of US$7,500 a year for education can be spent is 'broadly interpreted by the company' (line 34). What does this mean exactly?
   a) The money must be spent on training to be an interpreter.
   b) Education need not only mean formal study.
   c) Motorola must give its permission before the money is spent.

Overseas postings

Vocabulary tasks

A Synonyms

1. The writer uses the phrase 'trailing spouse' to describe the wife or husband of an expatriate executive. What other phrase is used in the article with the same meaning?
2. The text also refers to 'overseas postings' (line 13).
   a) Find three other words in the article with a similar meaning to 'posting'
   b) Find two other words in the article that could replace the word 'overseas' in that phrase.

B Words that seem similar

1. The words 'cite' (line 68) and 'site' (line 89) are pronounced in the same way but have completely different meanings. Match these definitions to the two words.
   a) mention or quote something
   b) put a building in a particular location
2. The money Shell spends on giving advice to expatriate couples at its spouse employment centre is very *cost efficient* (line 59). A similar expression is *cost effective*, but it has a slightly different meaning. Which of the following definitions fits the word *efficient* and which fits the word *effective*.
   a) producing the result that was wanted or intended
   b) working well without wasting time, money or energy

C Word search

Find a word or phrase in the text that has a similar meaning.

1. available employees from which you can select the ones you want (para 2)
   p..ool............ of p..otential......... e..mployees.....
2. going abroad to work for your company (para 2)
   o................... p...................
3. emphasise or stress an idea (para 2)
   u...................
4. reject an offer of a job (para 2)
   t................... d...................
5. in all parts of the world (para 3)
   w...................
6. pay money back to someone after they have spent their own money (paragraph 3)
   r...................
7. giving financial support (para 4)
   f...................
8. try to prevent something (para 5)
   t................... p................... a...................
9. bring an executive back from an overseas posting, usually because of a problem (para 5)
   r...................

Overseas postings

10 something that makes it difficult to do something (para 7)
o....................

11 show you have strength and may use it to get what you want (para 8)
f.................... your m....................

12 try to persuade the government to do something or to change a policy (para 8)
l....................

D Complete the sentence

Use an appropriate word or phrase from Exercise C to complete each sentence.

1 At the end of every month companies usually ....*reimburse*........ employees for travel expenses.
2 Some people welcome an .... because they learn more about the world.
3 In most democracies, companies and large interest groups .... Members of Parliament to try to influence government policy.
4 In tropical countries it is important to .... diseases such as malaria or yellow fever.
5 Most large multinationals operate on a .... scale, with activities in almost every country.
6 Most urban transport projects such as metro systems or light railways receive .... from central government.
7 We had to .... ten international managers last year due to family problems.
8 Lack of confidence can be a big .... to success in most careers.

Over to you

1 John and Mary Cooper are a high-flying couple in their early 30s. Both have very good jobs, but in different companies. John, who is an audit manager for an international firm of accountants, has just been offered an expatriate posting in Poland for two years, which he feels is essential for his career development. Mary, who is an investment analyst in an American bank in London, is also career-minded. What are their options? What would you do in their position?

2 You are a member of the Human Resources department of your company, which till now has had no clear policy about support or training for expatriates. Each person has been dealt with on a case-by-case basis. You have been asked by the chief executive to propose a company policy about expatriation, covering training, preparation and support for expatriates and their families, both before departure and while they are abroad. Write a report or give a presentation with your proposals.

UNIT 18 Returning home

Before you read

Discuss these questions.

1. Companies often pay a lot of attention to the problems expatriates and their families can have when moving to another country, but less attention is paid to the problem of returning home and coming back to the company. What problems can you imagine?
2. Working abroad to acquire international experience is an important part of an international manager's development. What do you think would be the optimum time to spend abroad at any one time?

Reading tasks

A Understanding main points

Read the text on the opposite page about two managers who returned home after working abroad and answer these questions.

1. The article describes the experiences of two managers working abroad.
   a) Which one enjoyed his time abroad more?
   b) What did he like about working abroad?
2. Which of the two men found the time abroad more useful for his future career?
3. How long did each person spend abroad?
4. What is the recommended length of time to spend abroad, according to Anne Isaacs?

B Understanding details

Answer these questions.

1. Why did Paul Richardson return to England? Choose from two of the following possible reasons.
   a) to get better education for his children
   b) so his wife could continue her career
   c) because the company wanted him to return
   d) to develop his own career
2. The two men had different experiences when they returned to the UK.
   a) Which man is now unhappy?
   b) What reasons does he give?
3. What did Andy Spriggs gain from his time abroad?
4. What recommendations are given in the text to ensure a successful return home?

When it's time to come home

Overseas postings can leave you out of touch with changes at head office, warns **Joanna Parfitt**

The chance to spend a few years abroad at the company's expense can seem like a dream come true. But if you don't take time to consider the impact your decision will have on your career, then it could turn into a nightmare.

In 1992, Paul Richardson was delighted to be sent to the Middle East by his financial services company, with his wife and their new baby. The opportunity to be a general manager seemed too good to be true. He would be able to exercise his talents, implement new strategies and use his outgoing personality to make the company lots of money out of local businesses. Five years later he had achieved just that.

'I was a big fish in a small pond and enjoyed the lifestyle immensely, but it was time to come home,' says Richardson. 'We now had two children, my wife was keen to pick up her own career and there was nowhere else I could go career-wise and stay out there.'

So Richardson came home. 'My achievements abroad count for nothing now,' he complains. 'I am now a divisional manager and work as part of a team. Being a tiny fish in a huge pond makes me feel really frustrated. My career has regressed.'

Richardson blames himself. His success abroad had made him arrogant, and he ignored the need to network and research the new job back in England before he returned. 'I wish I had been less naive and had thought ahead more,' he says. 'Two years down the road I am still unhappy.'

Andy Spriggs describes a very different experience. He decided to come back to England in 1997 after spending ten years abroad with Shell. He had been finding the expatriate existence 'shallow'. Integration with a local community was extremely difficult and he realised that there was 'always an underlying background stress'.

'Coming back to England was the best thing I ever did,' he says. 'Working overseas broadened my perspectives and the fact that I left Shell helped my employability too. Not only had I acquired an enormous amount of technical experience and a superb overview of the industry, but leaving such a top class organisation and moving to Arco Oil has illustrated that I am adaptable and a survivor too.'

Anne Isaacs, a director at Executive Action, a career development advisor to senior managers, believes strongly that time abroad should be considered carefully and worked into the career development strategy.

'Try to go away for no more than two years, or else you risk losing touch with new developments and your vitally important network of contacts,' she says. 'Unless you maintain contact in your home country you will find it really difficult to readjust and reintegrate on your return.'

> 'My achievements abroad count for nothing now. Being a tiny fish in a huge pond makes me feel really frustrated'

From *The Independent on Sunday*

C Understanding expressions

Paul Richardson decided to return because 'there was nowhere else I could go career-wise and stay out there' (line 27). What exactly does this mean?

a) No other country offered a better career for him.

b) To develop his career he needed to leave the Middle East.

c) If he had been wise, he would have stayed in the Middle East.

Returning home

Vocabulary tasks

A Words that create an impression

1 Paul Richardson enjoyed his time in the Middle East. What expressions are used in the article to indicate this positive feeling? (paras 2 and 3) *delighted to be sent abroad*

2 Now that he is back in England, Paul Richardson feels very negative. What expressions indicate this negative feeling? (paras 4 and 5)

3 In contrast to Paul Richardson, Andy Spriggs did not seem to enjoy his ten years abroad. What phrases give this impression? (para 6)

4 But Andy Spriggs found that his experience abroad was very useful for his career. He uses several words with the general meaning of 'very good' or 'excellent' to describe the benefit of those experiences. One is 'enormous'. What are the other two? (para 7)

B Understanding expressions

Choose the best explanation for each of these phrases.

1 at the company's expense (line 2)
   a) the company pays for everything
   b) it is expensive for the company

2 a dream come true (line 4)
   a) something you have always wished for
   b) something that is not real

3 too good to be true (line 14)
   a) it would be wonderful if it ever happened
   b) something much better than you expected

4 big fish in a small pond (line 22)
   a) someone who has all the power and can dominate others
   b) someone who is important but on a small scale

5 count for nothing (line 31)
   a) have no value
   b) lose money

6 two years down the road (line 45)
   a) two years as a travelling sales representative
   b) two years later

C Word search

Find a word or phrase in the text that has a similar meaning.

1. way you live (para 3)
   l..*ifestyle*........
2. want to do something very much (para 3)
   k....................
3. go backwards (para 4)
   r....................
4. proud and acting superior to others (para 5)
   a....................
5. lacking experience, thinking that people will be nice (para 5)
   n....................
6. something that is not deep or interesting (para 6)
   s....................
7. broad general picture of something (para 7)
   o....................
8. something that is very important (para 9)
   v.................... i....................

D Complete the sentence

Use an appropriate word or phrase from Exercise C to complete each sentence.

1. Many large companies run induction programmes for new employees to give them an ....*overview*............. of the organisation.
2. If you are using this book you are probably................................. to improve your English.
3. When choosing a new job or position in a company it is important to make sure your career will advance and not ....
4. Because people working abroad often have extra allowances such as free housing and low taxes, they can have a very nice ....
5. It is .... for the company to win that contract; we may go out of business if we don't.

Over to you

1. If you were going to work abroad, what are the positive benefits and experiences you would hope to get from this? What difficulties would you expect to have?
2. There are an increasing number of training courses on cross-cultural awareness to try to minimise the impact of culture shock. But the problems of re-entry and reintegration are often overlooked. Make a list of these problems. Then try to work out some policies or actions that a company could take to reduce these problems.

Glossary

English	French	Spanish
acquisition	acquisition, achat	adquisición
added value	valeur ajoutée	valor añadido
agenda	ordre du jour	orden del día
Anglo-Saxon	anglo-saxon	anglosajón
applicant	candidat	candidato
appointment	nomination (à un poste)	nombramiento
assemble	monter	ensamblar
assignment	tâche, mission	nombramiento
audit	(n) audit/(v) vérifier, contrôler	auditoría
autonomy	autonomie	autonomía
benefits	avantages	ventajas
boom	période de prospérité(n)	auge
boost	pousser, développer	estimular
brand	marque	marca
bureaucracy	bureaucracie	burocracia
bursary	bourse (d'études)	beca
cadre	cadre	cuadro
campaign	campagne	campaña
candidate	candidat	candidato
capital employed	mise de fonds	capital empleado
career ladder	plan de carrière	jerarquía profesional
career path	perspectives de carrière	trayectoria profesional
case study	étude de cas	estudio de casos
cash flow	flux de trésorerie	flujo de caja
chain of command	hiérarchie	cadena de mando
chairman	président, directeur-général	presidente
chartered accountant	expert-comptable	contable colegiado
coalition	coalition	coalición
code of conduct	code de conduite	código de conducta
collaborate	collaborer	colaborar
collapse	s'effondrer	colapso
commentator	analyste	comentarista
compensation	rémunération, compensation	compensación
compete	concurrencer	competir
competence	compétence	competencia
competitive edge	avantage concurrentiel	ventaja competitiva
components	composantes	componentes
comprise	comprendre, inclure	abarcar
compromise	compromis	compromiso
conduct transactions	mener, effectuer des transactions	emprender transacciones
conflict	conflit	conflicto
confrontation	confrontation	confrontación
conglomerate	conglomérat	conglomerado
consolidation	consolidation, intégration	consolidación
consortium	consortium	consorcio
core	principal	central
corporate culture	culture d'entreprise	cultura corporativa
cost-efficient	rentable	rentable
criteria	critère	criterios
cross-border	transfrontalier, international	transfronterizo, internacional
cross-fertilise	faire un croisement de	hacer una fecundación cruzada

German	Polish
Erwerb	nabycie
Mehrwert	wartość dodana
Programm	agenda
angelsächsisch	anglosaski
Bewerber	aplikant
Anstellung	wyznaczenie; mianowanie
zusammenbauen	zbierać; gromadzić
Anweisung	wyznaczenie, przeniesienie własności
prüfen	rewizja ksiąg, urzędowa kontrola, audyt
Eigenständigkeit	autonomia
Vorteile, Nutzen	korzyści; zasiłki
Boom, Aufschwung	boom
fördern	zwyżka; wzrost; podwyższać
Marke, Warenzeichen	marka
Bürokratie	biurokracja
Stipendium	bursa
Kader	kadra
Kampagne	kampania
Kandidat	kandydat
Betriebskapital, Nettogesamtvermögen	użyty kapitał
Karriereleiter	szczeble kariery
Laufbahn	kariera
Fallstudie	przypadek
Cash-flow	przepływ gotówki
Weisungshierarchie	zależność służbowa
Vorsitzender	prezes
staatlich geprüfter Bilanzbuchhalter	główny księgowy
Koalition	koalicja
Verhaltensregeln	zasady postępowania
zusammenarbeiten	współpracować
zusammenbrechen	załamać się; runąć
Kommentator	komentator
Kompensation	rekompensata
konkurrieren	rywalizować
Fähigkeit	kompetencja
Wettbewerb	przewaga nad konkurencją
Bestandteile	komponenty
bestehen aus, enthalten	składać się z
Kompromiß	kompromis, iść na kompromis
Transaktionen durchführen	przeprowadzać transakcje
Konflikt	konflikt
Konfrontation	konfrontacja
Konglomerat	konglomerat
Konsolidierung	konsolidacja
Konsortium	konsorcjum
hauptsächlich	głowny
Unternehmenskulttur	kultura korporacyjna
kosteneffizient	nie kosztowny; oszczędzający koszty, wydajny
Kriterien	kryteria
international	międzynarodowy
sich gegensetig unterstützende Maßnahmen ergreifen	wzajemnie się zapładniać (pomysłami, ideami)

Glossary

culture clash	choc des cultures	choque cultural
customercentric	qui privilégie l'aspect clientèle	orientado al cliente
customs union	union douanière	unión aduanera
decentralise	décentraliser	descentralizar
decline	diminuer	disminuir
delayering	écrasement des niveaux hiérarchiques	desestratificación
demand	(n) demande/ to demand : exiger	demanda
devise	concevoir	inventar
differentiated	différencié	diferenciado
direct marketing	marketing direct	marketing directo
discipline	discipline, matière	disciplina
discount group	entreprise de discount	grupo de descuento
distribution	distribution/répartition	distribución
division	division, service	división
down-to-earth	terre-à-terre	práctico
downfall	chute, effondrement	caida, ruina
drawback	inconvénient	desventajas
drive	dynamisme, énergie	campaña
duty-free	hors taxes	exento de impuestos
economies of scale	économies d'échelle	economías de escala
elite	élite	elite
entities	entités	entidades
entrepreneur	entrepreneur	empresario
establishment	les milieux dirigeants, l'establishment	figura consagrada, Establishment
exemplify	être un exemple de / démontrer, illustrer	ejemplificar
expatriate	expatrié	expatriado, desplazado
experiential	practique	práctico
expertise	compétence, savoir-faire	competencia
exploit	exploiter	explotar
flop	échouer	fracasar
flow chart	diagramme, graphique	diagrama de flujo
forecast	(v) prévoir-(n) prévision	previsión
foreign investments	investissements étrangers	inversiones extranjeras
freelancer	travailleur indépendant	trabajador autónomo
funding	financement	financiación
globe-trotting	qui parcourt le monde	que recorre el mundo
goals	objectifs, buts	metas
graduate	diplômé, titulaire d'une licence	licenciado
gulf	gouffre	abismo
headquarters	siège social	oficina central
hierarchy	hiérarchie	jerarquía
high achiever	jeune loup	persona de buen rendimiento
high-flier	cadre de haut vol	prometedor
hire	embaucher, engager	contratar
host	hôte	anfitrión
hybrid	hybride	híbrido
impetus	impulsion, incitation	impulso
infrastructure	infrastructure	infraestructura
ingenuity	ingéniosité	ingenuidad
innovative	innovateur, novateur	innovador
intangible assets	biens incorporels	activo intangible
integrity	intégrité	integridad
interpersonal	interpersonnel	interpersonal
IT (Information Technology)	informatique	informática

Glossary

Kulturkonflikt	konflikt kulturowy
kundenorientiert	koncentrujący się na kliencie
Zollunion	związek celny
dezentralisieren	decentralizować
zurückgehen	spadać; chylić się do upadku
Reduzierung das Verwaltungsapparat	usuwanie średnich kadr kierowniczych
Bedarf, Nachfrage	żądanie; popyt
sich ausdenken, erfinden	opracować
unterschieden	zróżnicowany
Direktvermarktung, Direktmarketing	marketing bezpośredni
Disziplin	dyscyplina
Billigkette	grupa dyskontowa
Vertrieb	dystrybucja
Abteilung, Geschäftsbereich	oddział
praktisch, nüchtern	osadzony w rzeczywistości; z nogami mocno na ziemi
Ruin	upadek
Niedergang	wada
Aktion	napęd, energia
zollfrei	bezcłowy
Größenvorteile	skala wzrostu
Elite	elita
Einheiten	jednostka
Unternehmer, Marktneuling	przedsiębiorca
Establishment	gospodavczego
ein Beispiel sein für	być przykładem
Expatriate	delegat
praktikal	praktyczne doświadczenie
Kompetenz, Fachwissen	ekspertyza
sich zunutze machen	eksploatować
einen Mißerfolg erleiden	fiasko
Flußdiagramm	wykres przepływu (gotówki)
Prognose	prognoza
ausländische Investitionen	inwestycje zagraniczne
Selbständiger	wolny strzelec
Finanzierung	finansowanie
weltreisend	podróżować po świecie (globtroter)
Ziele	cele
Akademiker	absolwent
Kluft	przepaść (metaforycznie)
Hauptsitz	siedziba główna
Hierarchie	hierarchia
jemand mit großen beruflichen Erfolgen	osoba wiele osiągająca
Überflieger	osoba o wybitnych uzdolnieniach
einstellen	najmować
Gastgeber	gospodarz
Mischform	hybryda
Impuls	impet
Infrastruktur	infrastruktura
Einfallsreichtum	pomysłowość
innovativ	innowacyjny
immaterielle Werte	środki niematerialne
Integrität	integralność
zwischenmenschlich	interpersonalny
EDV	IT (informatjka)

Glossary

jargon	jargon	jerga
jet-lagged	qui souffre du décalage horaire	que sufre de desfase horario
joint venture	joint-venture	empresa conjunta
link	liaison, lien	vínculo
lobby	faire pression	presionar
logistics	logistique	logística
loss of face	perte de face	pérdida de valor nominal
mainstay	pilier, pivot	puntal
maladjustment	mauvais ajustement	inadaptación
manufacturing	fabrication	fabricación
market share	part de marché	participación en el mercado
merge	(n) fusion/(v) fusionner	fusionar
misunderstanding	malentendu	malentendido
mobility	mobilité	movilidad
multi-disciplinary	multi-disciplinaire	multidisciplinario
multinational	multinationale (n.), multinational (adj.)	multinacional
myth	mythe	mito
networking	réseau de connaissances	trabajo en cadena
objectives	objectifs	objetivos
online ordering	commande en ligne	efectuar pedidos en línea
operational	operationnel	operativo
opt for	choisir, opter pour	optar por
organisational structure	structure organisationnelle	estructura organizativa
outlook	perspective	perspectiva
output	production	producción
outsource	sous-traiter	subcontratar
overseas	à l'étranger	exterior
oversee	contrôler	supervisar
overview	aperçu, généralités	perspectiva general
panel interview	jury d'entretien	entrevista de panel
participant	participant	participante
permeate	pénétrer	impregnar
personify	personnifier	personificar
perspective	perspective	perspectiva
pioneer	pionnier, précurseur	pionero
pitch	viser	orientar
pitfalls	pièges, écueils	dificultades
placement	détachement	puesto
plant	usine	planta
policy	politique	política
pool	réservoir	equipo
populace	peuple	población
post	muter, nommer	destinar, nombrar, enviar
prejudice	préjudice - porter préjudice à / préjugé	prejuicio
prestigious	prestigieux	prestigioso
production facilities	moyens de production	instalaciones de producción
prospects	perspectives	expectativa
pull off	mener à bien, conclure	lograr
pull the plug	abandonner	cancelar
qualification	qualification	preparación
qualities	qualités	cualidades
quoted company	entreprise cotée en bourse	empresa cotizada en bolsa

Glossary

Fachsprache	żargon
von der Zeitverschiebung durch langen Flug übermüdet	zmęczony różnicą czasu
Joint Venture	joint venture
Verbindung	więź
Einfluß geltend machen	mieć wpływy
Logistik	logistyka
Gesichtsverlust	niestawa
Stütze	główne
falsche oder ungenügende Anpassung	niedostosowanie
Herstellung	produkcja
Marktanteil	udział w rynku
fusionieren	fuzja
Mißverständnis	nieporozumienie
Mobilität	mobilność
multidisziplinär	wielodyscyplinarny
multinational	międzynarodowy
Mythos	mit
Zusammenarbeit im Netzwerk	networking
Ziele	cele
Online-Bestellen	zamawianie on-line
Handhabungs-	operacyjny
sich für etwas entscheiden	wybrać
Organisationsstruktur	struktura organizacyjna
Perspektive (auf etwas)	wygląd; prognoza
hergestellte Erzeugnisse	wynik; produkcja
auslagern auf Zulieferbetriebe	pozyskiwanie usług zewnętrznych
übersee, im Ausland	zagranica
beaufsichtigen, überwachen	kontrolować
Überblick	przegląd
Vorstellungsgespräch mit mehreren Vertretern des einstellenden Unternehmens	rozmowa (o pracę) z grupą pracodawców
Teilnehmer	uczestnik
durchdringen	przenikać
verkörpern	uosabiać
Perspektive	perspektywa
Pionier	pionier
zu einem bestimmten Ziel auf einer bestimmten Ebene ausbilden	tu: skierować do
Fallen, Schwierigkeiten	pułapki (metaforycznie)
Einsatz	lokata; inwestycja
Werk	zakład
Politik	polisa
Angebot	pula
Bevölkerung	ludność
versetzen	stanowisko
Voruteil	uprzedzenie; negatywne nastawienie
prestigeträchtig	prestiżowy
Produktionsanlagen	środki produkcji
Aussichten	widoki; perspektywy
zuwege bringen	tu: dokonać, przeprowadzić
die Zelte abreißen	wycofać się (z projektu; dosłownie: wyciągnąć korek z wanny)
Qualifikation	kwalifikacje
Eigenschaften	cechy
an der Börse notiert	społka giełdowa

Glossary

rank	rang	rango
re-accreditation	réhabilitation	nueva acreditación
readjust	(se) réadapter	readaptarse
recruit	recruter	reclutar
red tape	paperasserie	trámites burocráticos
references	références	referencias
regress	régresser, reculer	experimentar un retroceso
reimburse	rembourser	reembolsar
reintegrate	réintégrer	reintegrarse
relocate	transférer, muter	reubicar
repatriate	rapatrié	repatriar
replicate	reproduire	reproducirse
requirement	exigence, besoin	requisito
restructure	restructurer	reestructuración
retailer	détaillant	minorista
revenue	revenu	ingresos
rival	rival, concurrent	rival
salary scale	échelle des salaires	bandas salarias
schism	schisme	escisión
selection	sélection	selección
seminar	séminaire	seminario
set up (verb)	créer, établir, (s)'installer	establecer
share ownership scheme	plan d'actionnariat salarié	plan de titularidad de acciones
shareholder	actionnaire	accionista
soar	monter en flèche	elevarse
spectrum	spectre, gamme	espectro
sponsor	(v) sponsoriser – (n) un sponsor	patrocinar
spouse	conjoint	cónyuge
stamina	résistance, endurance	resistencia
subordinate	subordonné	subalterno
subsidiary	filiale	subsidiario
supplier	fournisseur	proveedor
sweatshop	atelier clandestin	empresa que explota al personal
take precedence	passer en priorité	tener prioridad
takeover	rachat, prise de contrôle	absorción
target (verb)	cibler	concentrar
tariff levels	niveaux tarifaires	niveles arancelarios
tax incentives	avantages fiscaux, incitations fiscales	incentivo fiscal
trade barriers	barrières douanières	barrera comercial
transact business	faire des affaires	negociar
turn down	rejeter	rechazar
vending machine	distributeur automatique	máquina expendedora
venture	entreprise, projet (n) - risquer, hasarder (v)	actividad comercial arriesgada
vertically integrated	verticalement intégré	integración vertical
vocational	professionnel	profesional
watchword	mot d'ordre	lema
wealth	richesse	riqueza
whistle-stop tour	visite éclair	visita relámpago
wisdom	sagesse, prudence	sabiduría
workforce	main-d'oeuvre, personnel	plantilla

Glossary

Rang	ranga; szereg
Ausbildung	nostryfikacja
neuanpassen	dostosować; regulować
engagieren	rekrutować
Bürokratie	biurokracja (dosłownie: czerwona taśma)
Referenzen	referencje
sich zurückentwickeln	cofać (się w rozwoju)
zurückerstatten	zwracać koszty; reimbursować
zurück integrieren	reintegrować
umziehen	zmieniać lokalizację
ins Heimatland zurückschicken	repatriować
nachbildern	replikować
Anforderung	warunek
restrukturieren	restrukturyzować
Einzelhändler	handlowiec
Einnahme, Einkommen	dochód
Konkurrent	rywal
Gehaltsniveau	skala płac
Spaltung	schizma, rozłam
Auswahl	wybór
Seminar	seminarium; wykład
einrichten, aufbauen	ustanawiać; zakładać (firmę)
Aktienverteilungsplan	program posiadania akcji akcjonariat
Aktionär	akcjonariusz
ansteigen	wznosić się (o kursie akcji)
Spektrum	spektrum
sponsern	sponsorować
Ehepartner	małżonek / małżonka
Stehvermögen	wigor, wytrwałość
Unterstellter	podwładny
Tochter-	przedsiębiorstwo zależne, filia
Lieferant	dostawca
Ausbeuterbetrieb	warsztat, w którym pracują wyzyskiwani robotnicy
vorrang haben	mieć pierwszeństwo nad
Übernahme	przejęcie
ins Visier nehmen	wyznaczać, wybierać jako cel
Tarifniveaus	wysokość taryfy
Steuervergünstigungen	bodziec podatkowy
Handelshindernisse	bariery handlowe
Geschäfte machen	robić interesy
ablehnen	odmówić
Automat	maszyna do napojów
Unternehmen	przedsięwzięcie
vertikal integriert	zależny
beruflich	zawodowy
Slogan	hasło; slogan
Wohlstand	majątek; bogactwo
Werbetour	seria szybkich spotkań w różnych miejscach
Weisheit	mądrość
Belegschaft	robotnicy

Key

Unit 1

Reading tasks

A 1 Functional structure, Organisation along product lines, Geographic structure, Matrix structure.
2 Yes, the functional structure.
3 During the 1980s
4 Reduce costs and take advantage of new technology. Result was less bureaucratic organisations.
5 A very flat organisational structure.

B 1 matrix 2 functional 3 geographic 4 product lines

C 2 negative 3 positive 4 negative 5 positive 6 positive 7 positive

Vocabulary tasks

A 2 g 3 h 4 a 5 f 6 i 7 d
8 e 9 b

B 2 software companies 3 product lines 4 project teams
5 business units 6 country managers

C 2 f 3 b 4 e 5 g 6 a 7 d

D 2 on 3 along 4 through 5 by 6 up into

E 1 See the *Longman Business English Dictionary*, pages 56–7.
2 See the *Longman Business English Dictionary*, pages 86–7, 286–8, 374–5.

Unit 2

Reading tasks

A 1 b) Ford c) Honda d) Honda e) Ford f) Honda g) Honda
h) Ford i) Honda
2 Due to rising costs, shared tastes in car styling worldwide and a need for economies of scale.
3 Ford replaced its functional departments with multi-disciplinary teams in 1993.
Honda decentralised and changed to a geographic structure.

B a) 8 b) 3 c) 5 d) 10 e) 7 f) 2 g) 4 h) 1 i) 6 j) 9

Vocabulary tasks

A 1 parent 2 car makers 3 vehicles

B 2 production unit 3 autonomy 4 requirements 5 chairman
6 comprise 7 self-sufficient 8 output

C 2 autonomy 3 chairman 4 output 5 requirements
6 economies of scale 7 production units

D 2 a large degree 3 rapidly 4 firmly 5 simultaneously
6 increasingly 7 such a high proportion

Unit 3

Reading tasks

A 1 China, Malaysia or Indonesia, because of low costs.
2 Because manufacturing in Europe and the US satisfies design and quality requirements better.
3 It gives more flexibility in case a plant needs to be closed or relocated quickly.
4 *Advantages*: they can be more easily moved from one country to another.
Disadvantages: production innovation, which is sometimes linked to manufacturing, may be reduced.
5 It gives a company more flexibility to supply differentiated products into different markets and to adjust to changes in costs.

B 2 F 3 T 4 F 5 F 6 T

C **2** Lego's
3 concentrating manufacturing in Europe and the US
4 the decline of trade barriers and the opening of new markets to foreign investment
5 the fact that costs can be subject to rapid change
6 a business or company

Vocabulary tasks
A 1 plants, manufacturing bases, assembly operations
2 manufacturing

B 2 manufacturing network **3** trade barriers **4** tariff levels **5** cost-driven approach
6 acquisitions **7** assembly plant **8** differentiated products
9 outsourcing **10** capital employed **11** sweatshop conditions

C 2 f **3** c **4** d **5** a **6** e

D 2 notably **3** links **4** eminently **5** augmenting **6** swiftly

Unit 4

Reading tasks
A 1 No – he see lots of difficulties.
2 Demand is growing in the main South American markets, especially Argentina and Brazil.
3 Colombia – it is not part of the Mercosur customs union.
4 It is the region's biggest market; the government gives tax incentives to high-tech industries; Dell's 'Brazilian' computers will have duty-free access to Mercosur countries.
5 c, e, h

B 2 T **3** F **4** F **5** T **6** T **7** T **8** T **9** F

C 2 other parts delivered from Brazilian suppliers
3 PCs are assembled to order
4 PCs are packed
5 PCs are delivered to consumers

D a) 4 **b)** 7 **c)** 1 **d)** 5 **e)** 3 **f)** 6 **g)** 8 **h)** 2

Vocabulary tasks
A 2 online ordering **3** venture **4** populace
5 challenge **6** volatile **7** red tape
8 animosities **9** attain **10** struggling

B 1 b) manufacturing venture **c)** import tariffs **d)** customs union
e) production volumes **f)** logistics system
2 b) serve a market **c)** generate wealth **d)** gain access **e)** meet criteria

C 2 mount ... campaign **3** production volumes **4** logistics system **5** import tariffs
6 meet ... criteria **7** serve a market **8** customs union

Unit 5

Reading tasks
A 2 T **3** F **4** T **5** F **6** F **7** F **8** T

B 1 b **2** b **3** a **4** b

C 2 cross-border deals **3** merger deals
4 a company's ability to create added value **5** what happens after the deal is done
6 deal makers **7** post-merger integration
8 executives who put deals together

Key

Vocabulary tasks
- **A** 2 takeover 3 go global 4 deal makers 5 cut costs 6 boost revenue 7 post-merger integration 8 posted
- **B** 2 a 3 a 4 b 5 b 6 a 7 b 8 a
- **C** 2 out of 3 on 4 to 5 in 6 to 7 to 8 in

Unit 6

Reading tasks
- **A** 1 c 2 b
- **B** 2 T 3 F 4 T 5 F 6 T 7 F 8 T
- **C** a) 1 b) 6 c) 2 d) summary e) 5 f) 3 g) 4

Vocabulary tasks
- **A** 1 b) outsourcing c) freelancers d) vertically integrated e) outside suppliers f) independent units g) open market h) economies ... scale
  2 corporation (only used for very large companies)
  organisation (a general word, mainly for big companies)
  firm (can be applied to any size of company, but often used for professional partnerships e.g. lawyers)
  entity (a legal term for a company)
- **B** 2 b 3 b 4 a 5 a 6 a
- **C** 2 work out 3 carry out 4 break ... up 5 transact ... with 6 affected by

Unit 7

Reading tasks
- **A** 1 Wal-Mart 2 colleagues 3 UK (Asda), US (Wal-Mart) 4 b 5 a share ownership scheme 6 terminology - speak the same language
  middle management must be motivated to feel part of the new structure
  getting to know each other
- **B** 2 F 3 T 4 T 5 T 6 T 7 F 8 T
- **C** 1 a 2 b

Vocabulary tasks
- **A** 1 staff 2 imposing one culture on another (line 62)
- **B** 2 collapse 3 replicated 4 tangible 5 legend 6 complacent 7 compromises 8 aligned 9 swapping
- **C** 2 f 3 b 4 d 5 h 6 a 7 g 8 e
- **D** 2 d 3 f 4 h 5 g 6 a 7 e 8 b
- **E** 2 product lines 3 sales assistant 4 business trips 5 IT systems 6 name badges 7 middle management 8 store manager

Unit 8

Reading tasks
- **A** 1 b
  2 a) T b) F c) T d) F
- **B** 1 b) Swiss, German c) British d) Swiss, German e) American f) French g) British
  2 British

3 German – a co-ordinated network of individuals who make appropriate decisions based on professional competence and knowledge.
British – a network of relationships between individuals
French – an authority network with differentiated levels of power

C 1 b   2 a

Vocabulary tasks
A 2 a   3 e   4 c   5 d
B 2 success-oriented managers   3 career paths   4 side-track   5 diminishing interest
C 2 d   3 e   4 c   5 a
D 2 differ from   3 have a ... feeling for   4 compete with   5 measure up

Unit 9

Reading tasks
A 1 Contrasting attitudes to managerial expertise and authority. Germans focus on technical skills and expert knowledge while the British focus on management skills. British managers frequently re-organise their departments, and frequently change jobs, which the Germans do much less.
2 b) T   c) F   d) F   e) T   f) T   g) F   h) T
3 The article is fairly balanced in its views, and does not come down clearly on one side or the other.
4 *strengths of the German pattern* (positive), *its ... stability* (positive), *rigid attitudes* (negative), *unstable and less technically oriented British pattern* (negative)

B a) 6   b) 1   c) 7   d) 4   e) 2   f) 5   g) 3

Vocabulary tasks
A 1 a) a big difference   b) gap, schism
2 top management (or senior management), junior management (not mentioned in the text)
3 a) present   b) position, post
4 finance, sales, IT, production, logistics, R&D, quality, administration, engineering
B 1 contrasting attitudes, different levels of qualification, major problems, constant change, rigid attitudes, unstable British pattern, less technically oriented British pattern, different career systems, different ways of doing business
2 b) a study   c) problems   d) change   e) jobs   f) a position
C 2 managerial expertise   3 career path   4 organisational hierarchy
5 partner company   6 routine problems   7 management rank
D 2 knowledge   3 organisational (or organised)   4 organisation   5 adjust
6 adjustable   7 collaborate   8 collaborative

Unit 10

Reading tasks
A 1 Generally positive, but not all are enthusiastic.
2 INSEAD, Harvard, Stanford, London Business School, Manchester.
3 No. Most are sponsored by their companies.
4 The US.

B 1 McKinsey, OgilvyOne Worldwide, PricewaterhouseCoopers, Shell
2 Not all MBA's are equal – there are differences in quality. For Shell, MBAs do not train people in technical leadership, which is what the company wants. PricewaterhouseCoopers are concerned that if you sponsor an employee to do an MBA they may then leave the company.
3 All but Shell are service companies in consulting, finance, marketing.

Key

C *Equally convinced of the value of MBAs is ... , OgilvyOne Worldwide ...* (positive)
But not every company favours MBAs (negative)
Companies like chartered accountants PricewaterhouseCoopers take a more middle-of-the-road approach (between positive and negative)

Vocabulary tasks
A 2 sponsor   3 jargon   4 networking   5 high achievers   6 ambivalent
B 2 h   3 e   4 a   5 b   6 g   7 c   8 f
C 2 raise its profile   3 have the edge   4 undertake an evaluation   5 develop a career
D *MBAs have not traditionally commanded the same respect in the UK as in the US, but an increasing number of UK employers are now taking them very seriously indeed.*
(Contrast between the attitude of US and UK employers towards MBAs.)

... the company still prefers MBAs gained abroad ...
Nevertheless, McKinsey is actively raising its profile over here ...
(Contrast between McKinsey's general preference for foreign MBAs and its growing interest in MBAs from the UK.)

... producing people who have a good overview of the business rather than a concern for details
(Contrast between two ways of looking at business problems.)

But not every company favours MBAs
(Contrast between companies who favour MBAs and those who do not.)

Shell's work is technical, while MBAs from leading schools are pitched at a more strategic level
(Contrast between Shell's training needs and the focus of many MBA courses.)

While it does not actively target MBAs ... a growing proportion of its senior consultants have them
(Contrast between PricewaterhouseCoopers' policy and what happens in practice.)

MBAs do bring a breadth of vision to the business problem rather than a narrow viewpoint ...
(Contrast between two ways of looking at business problems.)

Unit 11

Reading tasks
A 1 a
   2 b) T   c) T   d) F   e) T   f) F   g) T   h) F
B a) 3   b) 7   c) 1   d) 6   e) 2   f) 4   g) 8   h) 5

Vocabulary tasks
A 1 schools, college, universities
   university suggests a higher level or more prestigious institution; *school* is always associated with Business Schools, such as Harvard, INSEAD, London, Stanford; in France the *Grandes Ecoles* are more prestigious than most universities.
   2 recruit, hire
   3 recruitment drive
   4 a) some   b) approximately, around, roughly, more or less
B 1 qualifications, recruits, hire, recruit, recruitment campaign, recruitment drive, interviewer, interview, advertise, trainees, applicants, graduates, newly-qualified engineers, students, open day, job opportunities
   2 in the next three years, the early 1990s, over the course of the next few years
C 2 the early 1990s   3 Over the course of   4 schools   5 advertise
   6 Newly-qualified   7 applicants   8 interview   9 qualifications

D 1 automotive, electrical, marine, civil, nuclear, telecom, genetic
2 a) fall, drop, reduction   b) rise, increase, jump
   c) lack, shortfall, undersupply   d) surplus, oversupply, excess
E 1 h   2 d   3 f   4 a   5 g   6 e   7 c   8 b

Unit 12

Reading tasks
A 2 F   3 F   4 T   5 T
B 2 b, c   3 a, d, e   4 a, d, e
C intelligence tests, panel interviews, references, one-to-one interviews, personality tests, handwriting analysis, tests of communication, tests of social skills

Vocabulary tasks
A 1 selection practices, selection methods, selection process, selection criteria
2 capabilities, qualities, competencies, ability, personal qualities or characteristics.
3 Smart   – clever, well-dressed, intelligent, neat
  Willing – helpful, enthusiastic, eager
  Able   – competent, skilful
  Nice   – friendly, sociable, enjoyable, pleasant, beautiful, kind
4 Smart   – clever, intelligent
  Willing – enthusiastic, eager
  Able   – competent, skilful
  Nice   – charming, friendly, sociable, pleasant
B 2 whereas   3 similarly   4 in addition   5 though
C 2 e   3 a   4 f   5 b   6 c

Unit 13

Reading tasks
A 1 b   2 b
B 2 F   3 T   4 F   5 F   6 T   7 F
C 1 a   2 a
3 b) deductive   c) experiential   d) inductive
D a) 3   b) 1   c) 6   d) 4   e) 5   f) 2

Vocabulary tasks
A 1 on the other hand
2 a) rather than   b) as opposed to
B 2 loose   3 active   4 practical
C 2 conflict   3 voicing their opinion   4 debate   5 training
D 2 come more naturally   3 see ... point   4 perfectly natural
5 expense ... others   6 concerned   7 have ... lot ... gain

Unit 14

Reading tasks
A 1 a) London Business School Programme – 6 companies
        Ashridge Programme – 3 companies
     b) Lufthansa
2 b
3 In the UK, in English.

Key

B 1 b) T   c) F   d) T   e) F   f) T   g) T
    2 Europe, Asia and South America are studied. North America is not included.
    3 Ashridge: European Partnership MBA.
    4 Good for team building; a more relaxed relationship between lecturer and student; a 'modern approach' with a focus on leadership issues.
    5 They are more technical and accounting-led.

Vocabulary tasks

A 1 training programme, engineering group, working practices, management training, study programmes, business schools, business consortium, learning programme, multinational team, host company, learning atmosphere, team-building, management development, leadership issues
    2 programme
    3 a) jet-lagged traveller   b) whistle-stop tour   c) globe-trotting executive
    4 *top-flight executives* – a senior manager
        high-fliers – young, ambitious and talented people.

B 1 b   **2** c
C 2 c   **3** d   **4** e   **5** a   **6** f   **7** g

Unit 15

Reading tasks
A 1 c   **2** Just a few, 'a handful'
B 2 F   **3** F   **4** F   **5** T   **6** T   **7** T   **8** F
C 1 c   **2** b   **3** a

Vocabulary tasks
A 1 a   **2** a   **3** b   **4** a   **5** b   **6** a   **7** b
B 2 code of conduct   **3** prospects   **4** appraise   **5** salary scale
C 2 c   **3** a   **4** g   **5** e   **6** f   **7** d
D 2 appraisal   **3** consume   **4** consumption   **5** incorporate   **6** corporate
    7 transfer   **8** transfer   **9** succeed   **10** successful   **11** identifiable
    12 identification, identity   **13** measure   **14** measurable

Unit 16

Reading tasks
A 1 power and railway equipment
    2 Chairman
    3 the French state
    4 no – there are now French, British, German and Spanish parts of the company
B 2 T   **3** F   **4** T   **5** F   **6** T   **7** F   **8** F
C b) Ecole Nationale d'Administration   e) GEC–Alsthom
    c) Finance Ministry   f) Alstom
    d) CGE, later called Alcatel-Alsthom

Vocabulary tasks
A 2 d   **3** c   **4** f   **5** e   **6** a
B 2 h   **3** i   **4** l   **5** d   **6** f   **7** c
    8 k   **9** a   **10** g   **11** j   **12** e
C 2 make a decision   **3** reluctant to   **4** has its virtues   **5** bright
    6 attuned to   **7** in a tight grip   **8** rise up the ranks
    9 form a joint venture   **10** go straight to the point
D 1 bureaucrat   **2** Eurocrat   **3** Anglophile   **4** Francophile

Unit 17

Reading tasks
A 1 b
   2 **a)** effective   **b)** efficient
   2 Less popular because many couples have dual careers.
   3 Motorola
   4 Family breakdown or maladjustment
   5 Costs of repatriation, and damaged relations with local clients
B 2 T   3 F   4 T   5 T   6 F
C 1 b   2 c   3 b

Vocabulary tasks
A 1 accompanying partner
   2 **a)** appointments, assignment, placements   **b)** expatriate, foreign
B 1 **a)** to cite   **b)** to site
   2 **a)** effective   **b)** efficient
C 2 overseas posting   3 underline   4 turn down   5 worldwide
   6 reimburse   7 funding   8 take precautions against   9 repatriate
   10 obstacle   11 flex ... muscles   12 lobby
D 2 overseas posting   3 lobby   4 take precautions against   5 worldwide
   6 funding   7 repatriate   8 obstacle

Unit 18

Reading tasks
A 1 **a)** Paul Richardson
   b) He was able to exercise his talents, and implement new strategies.
   2 Andy Spriggs
   3 Richardson – 5 years   Spriggs – 10 years
   4 no more than 2 years
B 1 b, d
   2 **a)** Richardson
   b) His achievements abroad count for nothing. He is just a tiny fish in a huge pond. He is frustrated and feels that his career has regressed.
   3 It broadened his perspectives. He had also acquired a lot of technical experience and an excellent overview of the oil industry.
   4 The time abroad should be worked into the career strategy, and should be for no more than two years. While abroad you need to maintain your network of contacts at the head office.
C b

Vocabulary tasks
A 1 the opportunity seemed too good to be true; he enjoyed the lifestyle immensely.
   2 his achievements count for nothing; he feels frustrated, his career has regressed; he is still unhappy, two years after returning.
   3 he found the expatriate existence shallow; it was difficult to integrate with the local community; there was always an underlying background stress.
   4 superb, top class
B 1 a   2 a   3 b   4 b   5 a   6 b
C 2 keen   3 regress   4 arrogant   5 naive
   6 shallow   7 overview   8 vitally important
D 2 keen   3 regress   4 lifestyle   5 vitally important

Check Test 1 (Units 1–9)

A Complete each sentence with the correct word or phrase. The first letter of each word is given.

1. In the UK the service sector employs more people than the m................... sector.
2. The main office of a large company is called the h....................
3. Most publicly quoted companies have both a c................... and a chief executive.
4. The people who work for a company are called e....................
5. Wal-Mart is the word's largest r....................
6. In February 2000, Vodafone AirTouch succeeded in its hostile t................... of Mannesmann.
7. When it is approved, the m................... of Vodafone AirTouch with Mannesmann will be the world's largest.
8. In companies such as advertising agencies, people are vital intangible a....................
9. Subcontracting work to outside suppliers is known as o....................
10. The people you work with are your c....................
11. A person who does a similar job to you, but in another company is your c....................
12. The o................... is the total amount of products produced by a company.
13. Every company is looking for something which will give it a c................... e....................
14. When two companies merge they usually have greater e................... of s................... than as separate companies.
15. Because of the globalisation of business, an increasing number of mergers are c...................-b................... deals.
16. Some companies prefer to grow organically, but it is quicker to grow by a....................
17. Many government organisations are inefficient because they are too b..................., with too many rules and regulations.
18. PC manufacturers such as Dell and Gateway were among the first to sell their products through o................... o....................
19. The majority of start-ups and new v................... fail within two years.
20. F................... are people who provide their services on an individual and independent basis to different companies.

B Choose the best answer: **a**, **b**, **c** or **d**.

1. Multinational companies usually have .... in different countries.
   a) daughter companies   b) subsidiaries   c) factories   d) colleagues
2. One aim of all companies which sell goods or services is to increase their ....
   a) market part   b) market percentage   c) market share   d) market offer
3. In order to improve their services to customers, banks need to become more ....
   a) customer oriented   b) profitable   c) competitive   d) efficient
4. Having only .... in different countries gives global companies more flexibility to move their manufacturing activities from one country to another.
   a) subsidiaries   b) employees   c) research centres   d) assembly operations

5 Cultural differences are one of the potential .... of international mergers.
   a) threats   **b)** pitfalls   **c)** attractions   **d)** benefits

6 Most countries give foreign companies .... to attract new investment.
   a) financial discounts   **b)** important tariffs   **c)** tax incentives   **d)** share ownership

7 Companies that handle all aspects of their business internally, such as the big oil companies, are known as .... companies.
   a) multinational   **b)** venture capital   **c)** conglomerate   **d)** vertically-integrated

8 The movement of money into and out of a company is known as ....
   a) annual turnover   **b)** profit margin   **c)** cash flow   **d)** bank charges

9 All mergers aim to create .... for the two companies' shareholders.
   a) added value   **b)** lower costs   **c)** economies of scale   **d)** tax benefits

10 The Apple computer company has always been .... and different in the design and technology of its PCs.
   a) efficient   **b)** knowledgeable   **c)** expensive   **d)** innovative

11 Setting up a business in a foreign country involves a lot of ....
   a) import tariffs   **b)** red tape   **c)** tax payments   **d)** bank accounts

12 When companies decide to restructure, it is usually .... who are made redundant.
   a) middle managers   **b)** secretarial staff   **c)** top managers   **d)** production workers

13 To run their foreign subsidiaries, multinationals usually appoint a ....
   a) project manager   **b)** team leader   **c)** decision maker   **d)** country manager

14 In joint ventures, two or more companies .... on specific projects.
   a) collaborate   **b)** compete   **c)** practise   **d)** deal

15 One measure of a company's financial success is the return on ....
   a) production volumes   **b)** annual turnover   **c)** capital employed   **d)** profit margins

16 The use of share options to incentivise managers is becoming more and more ....
   a) reliable   **b)** widespread   **c)** expensive   **d)** tangible

17 One problem in international mergers is the difference in .... and benefits for managers with similar positions.
   a) duties   **b)** output   **c)** activity   **d)** compensation

18 Companies with very different products often have a structure based on ....
   a) functional areas   **b)** geographic spread   **c)** product lines   **d)** matrix management

19 When two companies merge they always look at ways to .... in order to be more efficient and profitable.
   a) recruit staff   **b)** cut costs   **c)** increase advertising   **d)** reduce salaries

20 Sometimes it seems that large companies change their organisation and carry out a .... process every few years.
   a) restructuring   **b)** decentralisation   **c)** merger   **d)** takeover

Check Test 2 (Units 10–18)

A Complete each sentence with the correct word or phrase. The first letter of each word is given.
1. International companies are increasingly looking to r.................. managers with an MBA.
2. An MBA is clearly one of the best q.................. for an international management career.
3. Many large companies s.................. their managers' studies by paying some or all of the costs.
4. While some subjects, such as law and management studies, are on the increase, others, such as engineering, are on the d.................. .
5. Because of the lack of graduates there will soon be a s.................. of qualified engineers.
6. Nearly all organisations use i.................. as one of their main ways to select new employees.
7. In Britain, many companies also use a.................. c.................., where candidates take part in a series of tasks and simulations.
8. It is also common in Britain for a new employer to request a written r.................. on candidates from their previous employers.
9. Organising people by different levels of power and authority is know as a h.................. .
10. When two companies merge it can be very useful to run t..................-b.................. courses to help people work well together.
11. Large companies that are famous, well established and generally successful financially are known as b.................. c.................. companies.
12. A c.................. is a large organisation that consists of many companies in different sectors.
13. A company with a good HR policy will carry out annual a.................. between each employee and his or her manager.
14. A person who loves France and all things French is known as a F.................. .
15. E.................. are people who are sent by their company to work abroad.
16. Young managers are less interested in working abroad than before because their s.................. often has a separate career.
17. Some assignments abroad can turn out to be a n.................., a really terrible experience.
18. Some managers consider time spent abroad as part of their d.................. programme.
19. Responsible companies will have an ethical policy and a c.................. of c.................., which all employees must follow.
20. Ambitious young graduates will look for a company offering good promotion p.................. .

B Choose the best answer: **a**, **b**, **c** or **d**.
1. A key international management competency for Unilever is entrepreneurial ....
   a) force   b) drive   c) strength   d) determination
2. Many organisations have a salary .... which indicates the salary for different jobs.
   a) level   b) ladder   c) scale   d) review
3. When two companies want to work together they often .... a joint venture.
   a) form   b) run   c) do   d) manage
4. .... is a word used to describe people who are clever and intelligent.
   a) Wise   b) Competent   c) Bright   d) Eager

Check Test 2

5 Young managers who have good prospects for quick promotion are often known as ....
   a) technocrats   b) globe-trotters   c) top-flight executives   d) high-fliers

6 The chief executive can be said to .... the company.
   a) organise   b) run   c) own   d) motivate

7 Training courses which include activities such as role-plays and simulations use an .... approach.
   a) experiential   b) academic   c) cognitive   d) deductive

8 In oriental cultures, to .... is one of the most embarrassing things that can happen.
   a) lose a job   b) make a mistake   c) lose face   d) receive a favour

9 The special words used by people in the same profession are known as ....
   a) slang   b) dialect   c) pidgin   d) jargon

10 When young people spend their first months in a new job on a training programme they are known as ....
   a) applicants   b) novices   c) trainees   d) students

11 Training that has clear applications to a job or type of work can be said to be ....
   a) theoretical   b) practical   c) interesting   d) cost-effective

12 It is very expensive to .... people who fail in an overseas job and have to return early.
   a) insure   b) dismiss   c) retrain   d) repatriate

13 People who are sent abroad by their company often have a better .... than at home because they have a higher salary and other benefits such as free housing.
   a) lifestyle   b) programme   c) career   d) placement

14 Most companies .... employees for their travel expenses at the end of the month.
   a) sponsor   b) support   c) compensate   d) reimburse

15 It is common for large companies and professional bodies to .... politicians and government departments to try to persuade them to accept their point of view.
   a) lobby   b) persuade   c) pay   d) entice

16 Some young managers .... overseas postings because their spouse many not be able to work in the foreign country.
   a) postpone   b) turn down   c) delay   d) prefer

17 Sometimes when people return from a period overseas they have problems readjusting and find that their career has .... instead of advancing.
   a) retired   b) turned down   c) regressed   d) broken down

18 Selecting the right person for an overseas .... is crucial but not easy to do.
   a) visit   b) mission   c) task   d) assignment

19 Because of long working hours and increased responsibilities, more and more managers are suffering from ....
   a) tension   b) stress   c) insomnia   d) frustration

20 In Anglo-Saxon cultures, companies test a candidate's .... : their ability to do the job well.
   a) personality   b) intelligence   c) skills   d) qualifications

Check Test Key

Test 1

A
1 manufacturing 2 headquarters 3 chairman 4 employees
5 retailer 6 takeover 7 merger 8 assets
9 outsourcing 10 colleagues 11 counterpart 12 output
13 competitive edge 14 economies ... scale 15 cross-border 16 acquisitions
17 bureaucratic 18 online ordering 19 ventures 20 Freelancers

B
1 b 2 c 3 a 4 d
5 b 6 c 7 d 8 c
9 a 10 d 11 b 12 a
13 d 14 a 15 c 16 b
17 d 18 c 19 b 20 a

Test 2

A
1 recruit 2 qualifications 3 sponsor/support 4 decline/decrease
5 shortage 6 interviews 7 assessment centres 8 reference
9 hierarchy 10 team-building 11 blue chip 12 conglomerate
13 appraisals 14 Francophile 15 Expatriates 16 spouse
17 nightmare 18 development 19 code of conduct 20 prospects

B
1 b 2 c 3 a 4 c
5 d 6 b 7 a 8 c
9 d 10 c 11 b 12 d
13 a 14 d 15 a 16 b
17 c 18 d 19 b 20 c